Touching

Marie-Louise von Franz, Honorary Patron

**Studies in Jungian Psychology
by Jungian Analysts**

Daryl Sharp, General Editor

TOUCHING

Body Therapy
and
Depth Psychology

DELDON ANNE MCNEELY

To my patients and my children—Romany,
Jonathan and Yseulte—who teach me so much and
indulge my absences to write.

Canadian Cataloguing in Publication Data

McNeely, Deldon Anne
  Touching : body therapy and depth psychology

(Studies in Jungian psychology by Jungian analysts; 30)

Bibliography: p.
Includes index
ISBN 0-919123-29-5

1. Psychoanalysis.   2. Mind and body therapies.
3. Jung, C. G. (Carl Gustav), 1875-1961. I. Title.
II. Series.

BF175.M26 1987   150.19'54   C87-094477-0

INNER CITY BOOKS
Box 1271, Station Q, Toronto, Canada M4T 2P4
Telephone (416) 927-0355

Honorary Patron: Marie-Louise von Franz.
Publisher and General Editor: Daryl Sharp.
Business Development: Vicki Cowan.
Editorial Board: Fraser Boa, Daryl Sharp, Marion Woodman.
Production Assistants: Ben Sharp, David Sharp.

INNER CITY BOOKS was founded in 1980 to promote the
understanding and practical application of the work of C.G. Jung.

Cover: William Blake, *The Reunion of the Soul and the Body.*
(See illustration, page 104, and text, pages 107-108.)

Index by Daryl Sharp

Printed and bound in Canada by
University of Toronto Press Incorporated

CONTENTS

Introduction   9

1   Physiological Origins of Depth Psychology   15
Freudian Psychoanalysis   15
Jungian Complex Theory   16

2   Body Therapy in Historical Perspective   21
The Cultural Background   21
Pioneers in Body Therapy   27
Therapists of Later Influence   43
The Contributions of Dance Movement   44
Contemporary Body Therapists   49
Personal Influences   51

3   Integrating Body Therapy and Depth Psychology   59
Introduction   59
Touch and the Analytic Model   62
The Meaning of Touch   67
Gratification in Analysis   69
Touch and Transference   76
Touch and Timing in Analysis   80
Body Therapy and Dream Interpretation   86
Touching and Analytic Training   93
Body Therapy and Jungian Typology   99

4   Experiencing the Unus Mundus   105

Notes   109

Glossary of Jungian Terms   115

Bibliography   117

Index   121

See final pages for descriptions of other Inner City Books

Acknowledgments

Special thanks to Bill Walker and Ann Mankowitz for their careful contributions to the articulation of Her message. I am grateful also to Tom Lavin, Marcel Gaumond, Arnold Mindell, Malcolm Brown, Clarisse Estes and Curtis Brooks for their support and suggestions, and to Eugene Monick and Gary Hartman for helpful critiques of the original manuscript.

I especially thank Lee and Joan for permission to use their material.

In 1925, D.H. Lawrence, poetic prophet,
has the risen Christ say:

*Dare I come into touch? For this is further
than death. I have dared to let them lay
hands on me and put me to death. But dare I
come into this tender touch of life? Oh,
this is harder. . . .*

—"The Man Who Died."

The Loving Touch.
(*Eros and Psyche,* antique sculpture. Capitoline Museum, Rome)

Introduction

In D.H. Lawrence's short story, "The Man Who Died," Christ awakens, bruised and emaciated, and is found by a young priestess of Isis. As she cares for his bodily and psychological wounds and nurtures him back to health, he comes to realize a whole new relationship to his physical body. At the decisive moment Christ must either acknowledge his bodily needs as his vitality returns, or turn away from this opportunity for relatedness . . . "Dare I come into touch?"[1] I take this to be a crucial question at this point in the evolution of psychotherapy.

Lawrence could be considered a prophet inasmuch as he envisions and anticipates in this metaphorical piece—written long before sensitivity-training, the women's movement and the self-examination going on now in the Christian church—issues of which psychotherapy has only recently become aware. He shows us a holy approach to the body; he gives us images for a healthy embodied spirit. He provides in this story a fantasy that leads us to wonder what our world would be like if the early church "fathers" had included some mothers.

Through the development and advancement of Logos—the logical mind—which Western man has accomplished through a progression of articulate and brilliant thinkers, we have sharpened our discriminative powers to analyze and dissect. We have taken the scientific spirit to its ultimate and now are in the throes of what Carl Jung called "enantiodromia." This term, borrowed from Greek philosophy, describes the moment when a force has reached its extreme and turns back on itself to become its opposite. We are seeing the great turning around from the dominance of the masculine values of Logos, the great analyzer and divider, toward the feminine principle with its values based on Eros, the great unifier and connector. Maternal religions are creation oriented, not achievement oriented. This emphasis on life-giving forces is necessary to maintain our planet. We are all agents bringing life into this analytic world.

The work to which psychotherapists dedicate themselves is about wakening life. It is about bringing life back to deadened psyches through the body, and to deadened parts of the body through the psyche.

Connection, relatedness, Eros, the power of touch—the effect of one person's body on another's is so great that we have had to deny it, ritualize it, repress it, then react against the repression in an attempt to integrate the wonder and glory of skin-to-skin communication into a vital place in everyday life.

There is a wide range of customs with regard to touching in human societies; for example, kissing seems to be indulged in more freely in the Mediterranean countries, Californians touch each other more casually and more often than do New Englanders, etc. Traditional artistic images of holding and touching are ubiquitous, attesting to physical contact as an archetypal need. I believe that in the modern world human beings could do with more touching; my practice reflects the fact that both children and adults suffer touch deprivation.

A stranger, a woman of about sixty, once made a deep impression on me. Sitting next to me as I held my baby at a church service, she reacted joyfully when my daughter spontaneously grabbed her around the neck and gave her an enthusiastic hug. "No one has touched me in so long," she whispered, "When you get old no one touches you anymore."

Physicians have learned that taboo, as have psychotherapists. The effect of touch is given minimal, if any, attention in medical schools today. C.A. Meier, in a fascinating account of the Asclepian healing mysteries, provides this amplification of the hands and fingers as healing powers.

> Rhea's fingers were caught in the maternal earth of Mount Ida. Her fingers became the Idaean Dactyls, who possessed generative power. Therefore they were accounted gods of healing, embodying creative power in the touch. The reader will remember the gesture of the outstretched hand in the picture of the creation of Adam in Michelangelo's frescoes in the Sistine Chapel. When Zeus healed Io of her madness by stretching out his hand over her . . . she gave birth, although a virgin, to Epaphus. From this Zeus derived the

epithet Zeus Epaphus, "he who touches." . . . Apollo as a healing god also uses the gesture of stretching out his hand over the sick person. . . . Healing by a touch of the hand is also implied in the names of Chiron and Dexion. . . . Chiron . . . (working by hand, practicing a handcraft or art; *Chirurg* = German for surgeon) has degenerated into chiropractic in our days. The idea that the finger possesses generative power no doubt underlies the German expression "to suck something out of one's fingers," meaning to invent or supply something.

. . . It is noteworthy that in Greek, hands and divine powers are equated . . . . kings and emperors . . . used to heal disease by the laying-on of hands, a practice continued until after the end of the Middle Ages by the English and French kings. . . . The gesture has been preserved up to the present day in ecclesiastical ritual.[2]

Depth psychology attempts to establish a dialogue between consciousness and the unconscious. It does so by an approach that utilizes symbolism, such as is found in dreams, fantasies, body language, art and ritual as a bridge between conscious and unconscious.

Carl Jung's empirical work was dedicated to understanding the nature of the psyche which enables the dialogue between conscious and unconscious. He showed that the psyche is structured around complexes. Complexes gather to a core a network of personal feelings, memories, images, behavior patterns and attitudes. At the archetypal core are found collective contents and behavior. Complexes tend to erupt spontaneously and interfere with ego-functioning. The task of the analyst is to assist the analysand in the discovery and resolution of interferences in his or her conscious functioning due to complexes, and to create new conscious attitudes subject to less disruption by the complexes. Archetypes are, according to Jung, manifestations of the Self; by relating to archetypes consciously the ego comes into clearer relationship to the Self and to one's own unique development or "individuation."

In the analytic work of bringing complexes into ego-awareness, the analyst focuses on their contents as they manifest themselves in images and somatic experiences. Like dream analysis and active imagination, body therapy can be an aid in uncovering the contents of a complex as well as a methodological intervention in promoting the transformation of a complex. Bodily expressions of complexes are essentially seen in gestures and autonomous behavior, but even more dramatically in the area of psychosomatic illness.

Until recently, little attention has been given to the somatization of complexes by analysts unless a patient displayed some pronounced physical distress. Most analytic work has centered on dream interpretation and active imagination. This bias or lack of attention to the bodily manifestations of the psyche can be understood in the light of Western philosophical development. Although a mind-body dualism was implicit in the thought of Plato (427–327 B.C.), it was Descartes (1596–1650) who originated a radical split between "thinking substance" *(res cogitans)* and "extended substance" *(res extensa)*. This split affected the way succeeding generations viewed the human being. The compatibility of Cartesian dualism with the Judeo-Christian world-view assured its survival. Seventeenth-century Rationalists, represented by Descartes, upheld the primacy of reason over bodily experience, and their prominence led to the philosophical Age of Reason, the so-called Enlightenment.

In the nineteenth century, in compensatory reaction to this devaluation of the body, the Romantics (for example, Schelling and Rousseau) exalted nature and devalued the thinking man who would sacrifice the instinctual life for the sake of cerebral processes. Nevertheless, the psychic-physical dualism survived this Romantic reaction and still prevails in our society.

Conditioned for generations to think in terms that separate mind and body, we find difficulty in understanding how complexes manifest themselves somatically. This difficulty inhibits psychotherapists from using more interventions which focus on bodily manifestations of the unconscious. I have spoken with analysts who do body therapy, and most find it difficult to combine analysis and body work in the treatment of one individual. Several analysts told me that they do body therapy with some patients and analysis with others, but few analysts combine these methods.

Since I studied body therapy before having had analytic training, it is vital to me to integrate what I know of the body into my analytic style; however, when I attempt to do so I encounter certain resistances in myself, which I believe mirror the resistance of the culture to the emergence of new attitudes toward the body.

If any theory should allow the integration of body therapy and analysis, it would be Jung's. Jung was interested in finding a way in which the mind-body dualism could be overcome and these opposites integrated. He conceptualized a psychophysical relatedness which provides an alternative to viewing either mind or body as the primary source of experience. Analytical psychology recognizes archetypes as spanning the instinctual-spiritual continuum. Archetypes, the nuclei of complexes, bridge the mind-body dichotomy at the psychoid level, offer a psychological alternative to the dualistic way of looking at experience, and make possible the compatibility of analysis and body therapy, both of which aim to unite the mental and physical and to integrate consciousness and the unconscious.

I use the term "body therapy" to refer to a process occurring between a person and a therapist who use bodily focus and movement to achieve their mutual goal: the discovery of heretofore unrecognized aspects of the psyche. The therapist uses bodily focus in addition to traditional attention to psychic processes in order to enhance the dialogue between conscious and unconscious.

Body therapy proposes two major methods of freeing the body and extending the range of movement and awareness. One is movement exercises designed to have the effect of opening spaces, stretching muscles and creating flexibility. The other is facilitating through touch the release of spontaneous movements that express deep feelings (i.e., complexes). Each of these approaches may be used in body therapy to evoke psychic awareness and make complexes conscious. On the other hand, either may be used to aid in freeing the body from rigidities without doing body therapy; that is, one can free the body from rigidities without dealing with the psychic material that accompanies that change. Whenever a fixed physiological condition changes, whether through exercise, laying-on of hands, biofeedback training, etc., there is bound to be a psychic change as well, but this may or may not be made conscious. Unless the psychological concomitants of such change are verbalized, and thereby made conscious, body therapy is not taking place—although the complex may change forms or a "transference cure" may take place.

There are many approaches to working with the body whose aim is simply to improve physical and mental well-being, without necessarily involving the goal of increasing awareness of the interior life, for example the physical therapies, aerobic exercise, massage, faith healing. Additionally there are approaches to working with the body which acknowledge the need for harmony between interior and exterior worlds, and which seek to promote that, such as Tai Chi Ch'uan, the martial arts and the techniques of Moshe Feldenkrais. In these approaches there is concern for self-actualization through centering awareness in the somatic sphere, but there is no intention to expose psychic contents or to create a dialogue between conscious and unconscious.

In what follows here, body therapy refers to any approach that focuses on the somatic expression of complexes, with the intention to reveal and transform the complex and so to extend the ego-Self interaction.

1

Physiological Origins of Depth Psychology

Freudian Psychoanalysis

Freud began his medical career as a biologist. His first published work was a report on animal neurology presented by his professor, Brucke, to the Viennese Academy of Sciences. His decision to marry in 1882 necessitated his abandoning the laboratory which he loved, in order to find more remunerative work. In that same year his friend Breuer described for him the curious cure of "Anna O.," whose symptoms had disappeared under hypnosis. At that time little account was taken of nervous diseases in Vienna's medical schools. Freud set out a course for himself which led to his attaining his ultimate desire of studying with Charcot, who was then the master of neurological disorders, at Salpêtrière, the "Mecca" of neurologists at that time.

In 1885 Freud arrived in Paris. There, under the charm and influence of Charcot, he decided to devote the rest of his life to the study of neuroses. Charcot called Freud's attention to a major malady of the time, hysteria, and to the importance of psychic factors in that disorder.

Charcot, an outstanding hypnotist, had successfully treated hysterical disorders, demonstrating the influence of the psyche on the physiological functions. Freud returned to Vienna, where with Breuer he continued to study the interaction of psychic factors and functional physical symptoms. The two concluded that neurotic symptoms were produced by the repression of painful memories or affects. They held that repressed experiences, apparently forgotten, influenced the personality unconsciously until brought forth again by hypnosis. Indeed, they found that if the childhood memories underlying the neurotic symptoms could be abreacted—remembered with emotion—the symptoms disappeared. Breuer and Freud published their findings in 1893, making the theoretical assumption that it was the presence of emotion along with the memory that had the therapeutic effect. The symptoms were considered to represent an abnormal form of discharge for quantities of excitation which had not been discharged naturally.

When it was found that patients who could not be hypnotized improved through the method of free association, psychoanalysis was born. At its inception, psychoanalysis depended on the realization of a relationship between psychic illness and emotional energy. Freud's biological training led him to express his understanding of psychic functioning in terms of physiological experience, and he was attracted to the concept of psychic energy. He assumed that excitation extended itself like an electric charge over the surface of the body.

Later Freud moved away from this emphasis on psychic energy and focused more and more on psychic contents and developmental theory, and it remained for Wilhelm Reich to continue the analysis of the importance of excitation and energy in psychic functioning. It was Jung, however, who further elaborated on the understanding of the unconscious, including *but not limited to* repressed material, by his development of complex theory.

Jungian Complex Theory

At the Psychiatric Clinic of the University of Zurich, Jung conducted a series of experiments on the associative process as a reflection of psychic activity. The basic procedure consisted of presenting a list of words to the subjects who were asked to respond to each word with an association—the Word Association Test.

These experiments showed that the reaction-time and quality of response to stimulus words indicate disturbances beyond the control of the conscious mind which manifest themselves only when the threshold of attention is lowered. The psychic association process reflected the presence and nature of emotionally toned groups of representations, which Jung called "feeling-toned complexes."

The Word Association Test proved the existence of unconscious influences and offered a way of investigating them empirically, for instance through reaction-times, blocking, falsification, and physiological measurements such as galvanic skin response and respiration curves. Jung showed that individual representations combine according to laws of association, but are selected and grouped into larger combinations by an affect.

Jung defined a complex as a nuclear element which is relatively uncontrollable. Connected with this nuclear element are a number of associations, stemming partly from innate disposition and partly from experiences conditioned by the environment. Complexes can resist ego control and split off from consciousness so that they function autonomously and against the will.

The ego, itself a complex, forms the center of consciousness; other complexes remain unconscious, or become conscious by associating with the ego. A complex can act upon the psyche without being recognized, and will continue to act until it is discharged, that is, the psychic energy stored up in it is transferred or assimilated emotionally. A complex which is only intellectually known is distinguished from one that is understood—made conscious in a way that renders it less likely to exert a harmful influence, its contents assimilated into consciousness, into the ego. Once a complex is made conscious it has a better chance of being understood and assimilated; in remaining unconscious, complexes can function compulsively and impair the unity of the psyche. A complex which has been resolved and assimilated emotionally results in a new distribution of psychic energy.

The process of making a complex conscious usually meets with resistance; intellectual understanding has no power over the complex, and only emotionally can it be transformed.

All complexes may show somatic or psychic symptoms, or combinations of the two. The presence of a complex can be detected in postural characteristics of the body as well as chronic emotional reactions, somatic symptoms, chronic or recurring illnesses and other physiological manifestations of tension. The ego can take these different attitudes toward the complex: total unconsciousness of its existence; identification; projection; confrontation. Only confrontation results in resolution, but confrontation usually requires suffering, for the complex remains unconscious because of conflict with ego values. When the conflict becomes manifest, the complex can be suffered through and resolved and the ego expanded, otherwise there are physical or psychological symptoms or both.

Let us see how this might look in life: A man responds lovingly to his wife until she becomes pregnant. While consciously he is happy about the prospect of becoming a father, he begins to treat his wife sadistically in insidious ways. He disdains her interest in her bodily changes, withholds his affection, and criticizes her in front of others in a joking way. She, not understanding this change in his attitude toward her, becomes anxious and more adamantly dependent, or angry, or withdrawn.

The pregnancy has touched a complex in this man. Probably he is reacting to some negative aspect of a mother complex. This may have its roots in his relationship to his own mother, but not necessarily. The archetype of the Great Mother, with her beautiful and terrible aspects and power over us, is part of every human being. While the wife enjoys participating, through her pregnancy, in this experience of the Great Mother, something about it antagonizes the husband. His ego does not recognize that he is caught in a complex; he may not even notice that his own behavior has changed unless his wife points it out to him (total unconsciousness toward the complex). If she does convince him that he has changed, he may refuse to admit that there is any conflict in himself between his conscious and unconscious attitudes toward her pregnancy; he may insist that there are good reasons for his new behavior, or may deny that it represents any real change, insisting that he has always felt negative feelings toward her (identification with the complex). He may even blame her for the changes in himself, attributing her distressed reaction to his coldness to "hormonal change" (projection).

On the other hand, he may listen and reflect on what she points out to him about himself. He then may confront the complex, and ask why he becomes sadistic when faced with pregnancy. He may find that his reaction is similar toward other pregnant women, to a less obvious degree. He may have a dream about it. Unless he can confront his own anger or disgust toward the mothering process, the complex will drain his energy, distort his ego-attitude (which wants a good marriage and a family) and cause discord in the relationship.

Freud and Jung agreed on the nature and effects of complexes, but only Jung drew a distinction between the personal and the collective unconscious. This divergence led to great differences in their theories. Jung's view was that since complexes are modal points of all psychic life, they constitute the normal structure of the psyche and are not pathological unless their existence is denied. Whereas Freud viewed the complex as a negative product of repression, Jung maintained that the complex has a dual aspect: while it is something to be assimilated, an obstacle, it can also stimulate us to greater effort and new possibilities. Jung also held that while some complexes have been repressed, others have never been in consciousness. The reintegration of a personal complex has a positive, healing effect, but the invasion of a complex from the collective unconscious is a disagreeable and dangerous threat to ego-functioning.

To return to the example above, if the husband decides to confront his negative feelings toward pregnancy, he may attribute them to his relationship with his personal mother. If there are negative feelings for his mother which are cleared up by bringing them to consciousness, this would be of benefit to him and would probably improve his marital relationship. But his experience of his own mother may be the tip of the iceberg. In confronting the dark side of the Great Mother archetype at the core of his complex, and in coming to see its ramifications in every area of his life—in his attitudes toward women, children, governments, food, sex, alcohol, his body, and his own creative processes—he may become depressed, even despondent. He then must grapple with his images of the negative mother within himself, if he is to avoid finding her in his wife or other personal relationships. To reduce this complex to a reaction to the limitations of his own mother or wife is to miss its fundamental meaning; to acknowledge that meaning would open possibilities of a new relationship to the inner life and to the spiritual Mother.

Often our life styles facilitate superficial change through which we avoid the meaning of our symptoms. This husband can get a mistress, a divorce, a hobby; he can move, become absorbed in painting the nursery, take an extra job to make more money. But the negative mother complex will continue to dominate this person's behavior until some transformation is brought about, perhaps through analysis and introspection, or by a trauma, illness or experience of archetypal proportions. As Jung writes,

> Psychic development cannot be accomplished by intention and will alone; it needs the attraction of the symbol, whose value quantum exceeds that of the cause. But the formation of a symbol cannot take place until the mind has dealt long enough on the elementary facts, that is to say until the inner or outer necessities of the life-process have brought about a transformation of energy.[3]

Only a certain number of complexes can be made conscious, and not all contents of any complex can be brought to the surface. In the end it is the state of the conscious mind and stability of the ego which determines whether the contents of the complexes can be assimilated without disorganization of the personality.

2

Body Therapy in Historical Perspective

The Cultural Background

Streams from many diverse sources converge into the deep pool of experience known broadly as body therapy. The main currents of body therapy flow out of modern dance; group therapy; music therapy; theater arts; holistic medicine; anthropology; experimental psychology; philosophical movements of the twentieth century (for example existentialism and humanism, and the focusing by Westerners on Eastern philosophies such as Zen Buddhism and Hinduism, especially Hatha Yoga); a generalized social movement toward acceptance of the body and away from the harsh attitudes toward the physical imposed by Victorianism, Puritanism and scientific materialism; and depth psychology.

These streams have met, touched and influenced each other. None can be said to be solely causal, but all contribute to a *zeitgeist* which is substantially different in its approach to the body from that of fifty years ago.

Astrology notes that in the precession of the equinoxes the twentieth century marks the end of the Piscean and beginning of the Aquarian age. In the second half of each age the influences of the opposite pole of the prominent axis are strong. Astrologists tell us that the Piscean age, approximately 250 B.C. to 1900 A.D., featured the growth of religions and ended in the characteristically Virgoan "age of reason."[4] The Virgo pole of the Piscean-Virgoan axis accounts for the progress made in hygiene and the healing arts during the eighteenth and nineteenth centuries. The Aquarian age is characterized, in part, by altruism and a focus on humane values, while science continues to flourish, especially in the area of communications. Some of the predicted influences of this age are the emphasis on the need for psychological regeneration through attention to the body, diet, health, and the prominence of the feminine in work, health and social service.

Whether or not one acknowledges any value in astrological influ-

21

ences, it is clear that attitudes toward the body have evolved dramatically over the past fifty years. In the late nineteenth and early twentieth centuries, repressive attitudes colored child rearing practices, clothing, sexual relating and treatment of the sick and dying. Freud, Jung and Wilhelm Reich examined these attitudes and rejected them, risking social and professional ostracism.

In the late nineteenth century there was a relaxed, tolerant attitude toward the child's body during the first years of life. However, at about the age of three or four, the "authoritarian father," a strict, rational-processing type, began to play a part in the child's education. J.L. Halliday, a public health researcher of psychosomatic medicine, suggests that this pattern was connected to the high incidence of hysteria in Victorian days; the strong influence of strict fathering in the oedipal period induced, perhaps, the use of the defense mechanism of repression in the child.[5]

The twentieth century brought significant changes. By the 1930s, while sanitary conditions were better for babies, psychological conditions were worse. Breast-feeding almost disappeared, feeding was by the clock, toilet training was imposed during the early months, modern furnishings and electrical gadgets limited exploration and freedom of movement around the house. With these changes psychosomatic illnesses in adults increased. According to Halliday, in the first half of the twentieth century:

> The life, instead of being allowed to unfold naturally with the concomitant maturing of bodily order, was subjected to an imposed system of conditioning which prematurely provoked, or predisposed to, bodily disorders by inducing tensional states or dysfunctions in the gastrointestinal tract, the respiratory system, the cardiovascular system, the voluntary muscular system, and so on. The third phase of infancy, however, was probably less frustrated than in the previous century insofar as more notice and attention was given to children; the phallic father was no longer in fashion, having been replaced at first by daddy (who was kind) and later by pop (who was ineffective, even contemptible); and there was less positive indoctrination of the sense of sin and guilt before an all-seeing and almighty God.[6]

The heavy hygienic curtain that enveloped Western society began to be pulled aside by the early depth psychologists and other questers. Anthropologists such as Mead and Malinowski brought back data about primitive cultures which confronted the world with some different social attitudes toward sexuality, presented the possibility of greater tolerance for the instinctual life, and challenged the notion that the only "correct" family scenario necessitated a dominant father and oedipal dynamics. Margaret Ribble championed the rights of infants and confronted the coldness of childbearing practices. Rene Spitz and Harry Harlow contributed evidence from experimental psychology on the part that physical closeness to the mother plays in the survival of infants and ultimately of the race.

Gradually the balance between patriarchal and matriarchal energies was shifting. The concern with control and power over the bodies of children was yielding to attitudes more concerned with feelings of warmth and closeness between child and parent. Through the new awareness fostered by social scientists, attitudes were emerging which challenged the strongly masculine, categorical type of thinking that characterized earlier scientific thought. Psychology, meanwhile, born out of a philosophical dichotomy that separated mind and body, was discovering and presenting the need for unity of the psyche, yet scorning the full meaning of that reunion. Edward C. Whitmont describes it thus:

> The subsequent devaluation—indeed the abhorrence—of the body and bodily experience which took place during the reign of the patriarchy, was part of the rejection of the magical and feminine dimensions. It culminated in the Cartesian mind-body dichotomy, and became the basic dogma for positivistic science. The concept was the starting point for psychology and psychoanalysis and effectively severed our conscious mind from awareness of the magical-transformation dimension. In consequence of this fact, ritual, in the course of patriarchal development, gradually and increasingly became ineffective and meaningless.[7]

One might say that during the nineteenth century the body had been conceptualized in mechanical terms, resulting in manipulative treatments of both body and psyche as a machine, for example through mesmerism, hypnosis, trephining and lobotomy. Indeed, the major part of the early psychoanalysts' attention to the body was in response to physical symptoms, especially those associated with hysteria (Freud, Bleuler, etc.). Jung's early word association experiments focused on the selective responses of the body. The analysts brought a new viewpoint; rather than bodily functions and illnesses being the result of mechanical actions from external sources, they were seen as functions of the whole organism's response to inner and outer influences. Georg Groddeck, a particularly colorful writer-physician, wrote:

> Whoever, like me, sees in illness a vital expression of the organism, will no longer see it as the enemy. It will no longer be his purpose to fight the illness, he no longer tries to cure it, he does not treat it at all. . . . In the moment that I realize that the disease is a creation of the patient, it becomes for me the same sort of thing as his manner of walking, his mode of speech, his facial expression, the movements of his hands, the drawing he made, the house he has built, the business he has settled, or the way his thoughts go: a significant symbol of the powers that rule him and that I try to influence when I deem it right.[8]

Many of the early analysts were interested in the expressive language of the body, as well as its pathology. In their overall attitudes it would seem that these analysts envisioned the body more as a mischievous child than as a machine—a child to be noticed, understood and brought under conscious control. Groddeck describes the "It," which is largely expressed somatically, as greedy and malicious, seeking its right to pleasure in good or evil:

> That does not prevent our looking like schoolboys when we are up against something we can't do, from wearing the same anxious expression we did in childhood, from showing always the same little mannerisms in walking, lying, speaking, which cry to everyone who has eyes to see, "Behold the child!" Watch anyone when he thinks he is alone; at once you see the child come to the surface.[9]

Cultural attitudes toward the body seem to be going through a transformation, from identifying the body as a machine (Descartes), and as a child (Rousseau and Nietzsche) to more recently as representative of the feminine. Contrary to the Western view, in the East the body as feminine is not a new concept. The Kundalini serpent-energy, which rises in the body in accord with different levels of consciousness, is considered to be feminine, and in Jewish mysticism, the feminine, the Shekinah, is the body-principle. While it is a step forward from viewing the body as a machine or an unruly child, seeing the body as feminine still reflects our incomplete developmental psychic process, in contrast to the possibility of focusing on body wisdom as an expression of the Self. Whitmont says:

> It is also erroneous to equate consciousness and ego with masculinity and the unconscious with femininity. This has been a tendency among Jungians based upon uncritical acceptance and superficial reading of E. Neumann's original statement. [10]

In *The Origins and History of Consciousness* Erich Neumann wrote:

> As the higher principle working through the head and consciousness, the ego comes into conflict with the body, and this conflict sometimes leads to a neurotic, partial dissociation which, however, is only the product of a later overdifferentiation. But even then the body totality seems to stand in a relationship of identity and equality with the totality of the psyche, namely, the self. These two totality formations, or images of wholeness, are superordinate to the ego consciousness and regulate the individual systems—including ego consciousness—from a total standpoint of which the ego can become only partially conscious. [11]

Here we have a clear statement of the reality that is slowly coming to consciousness in the objective psyche: the body totality seems to stand in a relationship of identity and equality with the totality of the psyche, the Self.

In this regard, Jung's psychology can be a major container for the ascension of the body out of darkness and one-sidedness and into wholeness. More will be said about Jung's contribution to the value of body work later.

During the era when patriarchal values of reason, control and white-male dominance predominated, the wisdom of the body was largely ignored. All that was not masculine was also ignored. We could say that the body, along with the feminine, homosexuality and dark skin pigmentation, were shoved into the background of

Western society and incarnated as shadow. In *Freud and the Post-Freudians,* J.A.C. Brown says:

> Epithets such as "mummy's boy," "soppy," "milksop," or "crybaby," reveal antifeminist tendencies when contrasted with the idealization of toughness, aggressiveness, and hardness, which are regarded as praiseworthy. . . . This type of character formation is in part the result of a reaction against the early weaning habits of modern times—it is a revenge upon and repudiation of the weaning mother.[12]

In the early analytic period a tolerance for the feminine principle and for homosexuality was most rare. As Groddeck put it:

> One might think that an age that is proud of its civilization . . . must know that on the other side of the Aegean Sea, in Asia, open pederasty is the rule. . . . Obviously [the church] derives this prohibition from the Old Testament, the whole spirit of which was directed toward bringing all sexual activity into direct association with the begetting of children . . . in this matter an evil has long been made out of what is a hereditary right. . . .
>
>   I was born at a time when people behaved as though . . . women had no sensuality in their nature. In the support it gave to this view one might say the last century was almost ridiculous, but unfortunately the results of this absurdity are serious.[13]

Today we are in a period in which the body is acknowledged both as a representation of the feminine and a point of contact with the unconscious. Several analysts have written about the emergence of the feminine in the objective psyche, such as Whitmont *(Return of the Goddess),* Sylvia Brinton Perera *(Descent to the Goddess)* and Jean Shinoda Bolen *(Goddesses in Every Woman).* This movement of coming to consciousness of feminine values accompanies a new attitude of acceptance and respect for the body. The "return of the goddess" is a phase of cultural development during which traditional masculine expressions of what is deemed right and good are being balanced by a flexibility and openness to the feminine voice operating in the world at large. Consequently we are seeing a concomitant movement, a greater awareness of the body in the field of psychotherapy; but among analysts, as in the larger collective, that movement still encounters some resistance.

Whitmont believes that in today's psychotherapeutic milieu the interpretive method alone is insufficient to bring about personality change:

> Whether this [is] because a revaluation of sexual mores and a new relation to spiritual meaning has to be dealt with first, or because the quality of our psychic awareness has since undergone a change, or, as I believe, because of both developments, our present psychological state increasingly calls for feeling and body awareness in addition to understanding. . . . The dominant attitude of this past cultural phase has been Apollonian and patriarchal; it has been a culture of abstraction, thought, and distance. It has tended to cut individuals off from their matrix; from instincts and affects; from nature, earth; from the body and the containing community.[14]

It is difficult to see how the next step will unfold, but we can hope for attitudes toward the body which go beyond our current conceptualizations.

In chapter three, I will explore some options that depth psychology holds open toward a more balanced integration of the body in analysis, but first let us look at some of the forces of attitudinal change in more detail.

Pioneers in Body Therapy

I consider the pioneers of body therapy to be Freud, Sandor Ferenczi, Alfred Adler, Groddeck, Wilhelm Reich and Jung. Naturally they were influenced by others: Nietzsche, Kretschmer, Krafft-Ebing, Schiller, the anthropologists, etc. I begin with these six psychotherapists because their primary concern regarding the body was distribution of energy (as seen especially in the drive theory). Over this subject they were found to come together, dissent and then separate.

Sigmund Freud

Freud's career exemplifies the movement in attitudes toward the body that occurred in the collective during the past century. He began as a physiologist examining the body at the most basic level, then moved to the study of neuropathy, concentrating on the nervous system.

At the time Freud began these studies the only orthodox therapies were those that treated the body as a machine. Electrotherapy was the treatment of choice in the textbooks of the day. Realizing the ineffectiveness of such an approach, Freud moved on to the field of psychotherapy using hypnosis, a methodology that manipulated the patient but which recognized the relevance of the psyche. His final position as psychoanalyst and his method of free association reflected an attitude of respectful observation of the whole person and the encouragement to disclosure.[15]

Only the most aware medical professionals of his day, such as Georg Groddeck, his contemporary and admirer, appreciated Freud's leadership in this movement from mechanistic therapy to depth analysis. Groddeck expressed his respect for Freud openly:

> In analyzing, I do no differently from what I did before, when I ordered hot baths, gave massage, and issued masterful commands, all of which I still do. . . . My treatment, insofar as it is different from what it used to be, consists of the attempt to make conscious the unconscious complexes of the "It." . . . That is certainly something new, but it originated not with me, but with Freud; all that I have done in the matter is to apply this method to organic disease.[16]

The resistance in society to what was being disclosed was formidable. Freud and his colleagues were discovering that morality and neurosis were related. In some way the energy of the mind-body unit was capable of being misdirected into bodily symptoms, in effect saying that a sick or disturbed body indicates a disturbed psyche that needs healing. This was not a popular message. Gerard Lauzun in his biography of Freud wrote:

> Not only Germany, where official science relegated Freud to ignominy and disgust, but the whole world, accused psychoanalysts of the most dangerous tolerance, of being obsessed with sex and of ruining society by turning everybody's eyes toward indecency and perversion.[17]

In addition to having his theories attacked for being arbitrary and artificial, Freud was associated with the "licentiousness of the Viennese," and the "carnality of the Jews,"[18] because of statements such as the following in 1908:

The position sanctioned by every authority, that sexual abstinence is not harmful and not difficult to maintain, has also obtained a good deal of support from physicians. It may be said that the task of mastering such a mighty impulse as the sexual instinct is one which may well absorb all the energies of a human being. Mastery through sublimation, diverting the sexual energy away from its sexual goal to higher cultural aims, succeeds with a minority, and with them only intermittently; while the period of passionate youth is precisely that in which it is most difficult to achieve. Of the others, most become neurotic or come to grief.[19]

Freud's original view of the instinctual energy of the body was that there was one basic drive present at birth. It developed through several stages, focusing on various erogenous zones and culminating in genital sexuality. Corresponding to the physiological development, the child's attention and strongest perceptual orientation were drawn to the needs of the erogenous zone which predominated at each stage of development. The psyche paralleled the body in interest and goal orientation.

In the interest of formulating the most parsimonious and least complex explanation of libido, and in order to have the most scientifically clean and biologically provable theory, Freud strove to keep this viewpoint foremost and to find experiences of patients to exemplify it. In this effort he was supported by Reich and Groddeck but criticized by Adler and Jung, who both felt he exaggerated the importance of the libidinal drives. As time went on Freud came to modify his original dogmatic viewpoint, and in doing so moved closer to Adler and Jung. But it was too late and not enough to bridge their schisms. It alienated Reich, who persisted in the most narrow view of the nature of psychophysiological energetics.

The first modification Freud made in his original theory of libido was to acknowledge the differentiation of an aggressive (death) drive from the sexual (life) drive, necessitating the dual-instinct theory called Eros and Thanatos. The dreams of shell-shocked soldiers of World War One forced this new consideration of the insufficiency of the old meaning of libido. This came closer to Adler's emphasis on the primary power drive, though of course to Adler aggression meant life, not death. Reich disagreed with Freud, seeing aggression as a healthy aspect of the sex drive and frustrated sexuality as the source of destructive uses of aggression.[20]

Later Freud focused more on the three components of the personality—id, ego and superego—which further changed the drive theory. In 1923, in "The Ego and the Id," he described the Id as a chaos, a caldron of seething emotions, being based in the somatic realm from which it has received the instinctive needs which find psychic expression in the Id.[21] (The term Id, taken from Nietzsche's *das Es* (the It), was first used by Groddeck, then adopted in the Latin spelling by Freud). The Id consisted of accumulated undifferentiated energy arising from the life and death instincts, about which Freud wrote:

> Only the work of analysis, by rendering them conscious, is capable of situating them in the past and depriving them of their energy-charges; it is just on this result that, in part, the therapeutic effect of analytical treatment depends.[22]

The ego came to be regarded as a reservoir of "narcissistic libido," energy cathected to one's self, which conceptualization made possible the distinction between transference neuroses, which were treatable by psychoanalysis, and narcissistic disorders (dementia praecox or schizophrenia, paranoias, melancholia) which were not. Freud now conceptualized the instinct of self-preservation, in addition to instincts of sex and death. In his 1922 paper on libido theory, Freud states:

> C.G. Jung attempted to resolve this obscurity along speculative lines by assuming that there was only a single primal libido which could be either sexualized or desexualized and which therefore coincided in its essence with mental energy in general. This innovation was methodologically disputable, caused a great deal of confusion, reduced the term "libido" to the level of a superfluous synonym and was still confronted in practice with the necessity for distinguishing between sexual and asexual libido. The difference between the sexual instincts and instincts with other aims was not to be got rid of by means of a new definition.[23]

Later in the same paper he says,

> It thus seemed on the face of it as though the slow process of psychoanalytic research was following in the steps of Jung's specu-

lation about a primal libido, especially because the transformation of object-libido into narcissism necessarily carries along with it a certain degree of desexualization, or abandonment of the specifically sexual aims. Nevertheless, it has been borne in mind that the fact that the self-preservative instincts of the ego are recognized as libidinal does not necessarily prove that there are no other instincts operating in the ego.[24]

In seeing anxiety as a warning, originating in the ego, instead of a symptom of dammed-up sexual energy, Freud caused a greater rift with Reich.

The third personality part, the superego, was thought to come into being through a process of identification with the parental ego.

Freud described the ego as a "body ego," but his conceptualization of resistances was entirely in the realm of mental defense mechanisms, which have never been clearly translated into physiological terms.

Throughout the confusion and dissension among these theorists Freud appears to have arrived at, maintained and established a consistent technique of having patients lie on a couch, not seeing and not being touched by the analyst. Lauzun tells us:

> The patient lay down with his eyes shut and was told to concentrate on such and such a symptom and to try to detect its source. If the patient remained silent Freud added "a little suggestion" by pressing his hand on the patient's forehead and assuring him that the thought would come. He also asked questions and insisted on everything being brought out in words even if it was something unpleasant, irrelevant, or banal. During the treatment of Fraulein Elizabeth, the patient explained one day that these interruptions and interferences on the physician's part were a hindrance to her, breaking off the flow of memories. The method of free association was born of this demand. Freud realized that the physician should interfere as little as possible and refrain from evoking any awareness of outward reality, whether in the form of events or of people, while the patient was mentally roaming in search of his or her own crucial experiences.[25]

According to Freud himself, "The physician should be impenetrable to the patient, and like a mirror, reflect nothing but what is shown to him."[26]

Sandor Ferenczi

Ferenczi, one of Freud's most faithful disciples, was more experimental. While Freud disapproved of Ferenczi's innovations, there was never an open break between them as with Adler or Jung. Ferenczi's changes were significant since they sought to shorten the duration of analysis by depriving the analysand of any form of gratification. The patient was urged to avoid sex, to take as little time as possible for elimination, and not to eat or drink for pleasure. Denying the gratification of libido was thought to leave more energy available for abreaction during analysis.

When these precautions proved of doubtful benefit, Ferenczi tried the opposite tack. He took the role of a good parent, even to the point of freely admitting his own defects to the patient. He permissively encouraged the patient to dramatize his or her memories while the analyst entered the fantasy play. Freud especially disapproved of Ferenczi's kissing patients. Ferenczi was the first to emphasize the importance of countertransference and the interpersonal aspect of the analytic procedure. As such he laid the foundation for psychodrama.[27]

With Ferenczi's thought there arose a crucial issue concerning the nature of the healing process. Freud thought that the bringing to consciousness of the contents of the unconscious was the essential factor in the cure. However, William Goodheart has suggested that Freud used the concept of the transference to defend against the full realization of the interpersonal impact between himself and his patients.[28]

Ferenczi's insight was that the patient not only brought repressed material to consciousness, but reenacted his infantile experiences in a more permissive and tolerant parental atmosphere. This insight has gained a lot of acceptance today, although the importance of the therapist as parent—that is, the reliving of repressed material— varies in the view of different schools, and even among therapists of the same school.

For example, some analysts stress the consistency with which the therapist holds to the symbolic approach, seeing this as containing and ego-enhancing, the primary healing factor in the interaction.

Others see the containing in terms of emotional acceptance and consistency to be primary. Still others, such as behavior therapists, focus on the therapist-parent's capacity to recondition response while the patient reexperiences his or her dependency with the therapist. In so doing, they believe, they enable the patient to maintain a more open attitude toward learning than the patient can achieve alone.

Alfred Adler

Adler, originally attracted to Freud's biological approach, had a long-standing interest in the capacity of the body to compensate for organic damage. Adler believed that compensation occurred in the psychological as well as physiological spheres. His concept of organ inferiority was later replaced by the broader concept of social inferiority. His attention to physical defects and bodily expressions of character traits was an important contribution to the evolution of body therapy.

> The bodily postures and attitudes always indicate the manner in which an individual approaches his goal. A person who goes straight on shows courage, whereas an adult who is anxious and hesitant has a style of life that prohibits direct action and something of a detour appears in every action.[29]

He also commented on the meaning of sleep postures:

> When we see a person sleeping upon the back, stretched out like a soldier at attention, it is a sign that he wishes to appear as great as possible. If he lies curled up like a hedgehog. . . he is probably cowardly. A person who sleeps on his stomach betrays stubbornness and negativity.[30]

On posture, insomnia, enuresis, sexual dysfunction and other examples of "organ dialect," Adler noted:

> The refusal of normal functions may be an expression of defiance; pain, an expression of jealousy and desire; insomnia, of ambition; over-sensitivity, anxiety, and nervous organic disorders, of craving for power. . . . A mental tension affects both the central nervous system and the autonomic nervous system. Where there is tension

there is action in the central nervous system . . . by means of the autonomic nervous system the tension is communicated to the whole body. . . . The body through the autonomic nervous system, the vagus nerve, and endocrine variations, is set into movement which can manifest itself in alterations of the blood circulation, of the secretions, the muscle tonus, and of almost all the organs. As temporary phenomena the changes are natural and only show themselves differently according to the style of life of the person concerned. If they persist, one speaks of functional organ neuroses. These, like the psychoneuroses, owe their origin to a style of life which, in the case of failure, shows an inclination to retreat from the problem at hand and to safeguard this retreat by clinging to the bodily and psychological shock symptoms which have arisen. This is the way the psychological process reflects itself in the body.[31]

Adler's detailed focus on expressive movement, his emphasis on the importance of social feeling and on the aggressive drive—which he defined as "fighting for satisfaction"—were important sources for the development of the holistic approach and psychosomatic medicine. As the dance therapist Liljan Espanek comments:

His first close linking of the organic functioning to that of the mind and emotion, and its interdependence, is the first premise for successfully using the body approach to influence the two other systems as is done in dance therapy. . . . The work with the body in movement demonstrates constantly this original life energy, the animal aggression drives, as an original biological force, which, when absent, leaves the human being passive, lifeless and disinterested in living.[32]

Adler, Groddeck and Reich all specified body language and interpreted disease psychologically, but their notions of the origin of the initial tension were quite different. For Adler, specific tensions were derived from heredity, history and the final goals of the individual, and especially the will to power. For Groddeck and Reich, tension was always a result of frustrated sexual energy.

Georg Groddeck

Groddeck intuited the psychoanalytic method and met Freud after conceiving of the It *(das Es),* which expresses itself through the fate of the individual.

I came by chance upon the idea that in addition to the unconscious of the thinking brain, there is an analogous unconscious of other organs, cells, tissues, etc.; and that through the intimate connections of these separate unconscious units with the organism as a whole, a beneficial influence may be directed upon the individual units by means of the analysis of the brain unconscious.[33]

Groddeck, as physician and director of a sanitarium, was a pioneer in the fields of psychosomatic medicine and psychoanalysis. As pointed out above, he saw illness as a form of communication. Some examples of his style are:

In attacking the tooth, the It is saying, in the gentle but persistent voice of the unconscious, "Do not chew; be cautious, spit out what you would like to eat. . . ." For the unconscious, a tooth is a child.

Bleeding of every kind . . . has a close connection with imagined births.

People who hate their mothers create no children for themselves, and that is so far true that we may postulate of a childless marriage, without further inquiry, that one of the two partners is a mother-hater.[34]

As far as I can tell, Groddeck limited his technique, like Freud, to verbal interpretation of his patients' symbolic language.

Wilhelm Reich

Reich deviated from the Freudian stance in making direct contact with patients, like Ferenczi, but on a much deeper level. Like Adler, Reich focused attention on body tensions as expressions of habitual emotional states, but carried his observations much further than Adler:

The difference between my technique and Adler's characterological attempts was that it consisted in character-analysis through analysis of the sexual behavior. Adler, however, had said: "Analysis not of the libido, but of the character." My conception of the character armor has nothing in common with Adler's formulations of individual character traits. Any such comparison of the sex-economic theory of structure with Adler's characterology would betray a fundamental misconception. Character traits such as "inferiority feelings" or "will to power" are only superficial manifestations of the armoring process in the biological sense, i.e., in the sense of vegetative inhibition of vital functioning. . . .

Adler rejected the sexual etiology of the neuroses when he became aware of guilt feelings and aggression. He ended up as a finalistic philosopher and social moralist.

Jung had generalized the concept of libido to such an extent as to make it completely lose its meaning of sexual energy. He ended up with the "collective unconscious" and, with that, in mysticism. . . .

Ferenczi, that talented and outstanding person, was perfectly aware of the sad state of affairs in therapy. He looked for a solution in the somatic sphere and developed an "active technique" directed at the somatic tension states. But he did not know the stasis neurosis and failed to take the orgasm theory seriously.[35]

Like Freud, Adler and Jung, Reich (from his earliest work in orgasm theory) had been on the track of the basic biopsychological energy which becomes manifest in somatic, mental and emotional states. He described its damming-up as resulting in impotence and its "streaming" in the full surrender of orgasm. He traced the locations where libido was blocked, first in the character armor and then in the muscular armor.

Reich believed that the tensions of "character armor" must be attacked directly. By character armor he meant chronic physiological rigidities corresponding to emotional barriers against feeling excitement. He distinguished between his analytic interpretive work, which he called "character analysis," and direct body-contact work on the defensive musculature, which he called "vegetotherapeutic treatment of muscular attitudes" and "character analysis in the realm of biophysical functioning."[36]

His method was to have patients undress and lie on a couch. He began by observing the breathing patterns. Reich envisioned seven rings of muscular armoring which transversely cut across the body from front to back: 1) eye area; 2) mouth and jaw; 3) neck; 4) chest; 5) diaphragm; 6) central abdomen; and 7) pelvis. He systematically attacked each ring by various techiques of exercise and massage. He called this vegetative therapy because of the powerful impact on the patient's deepest core of being, at the level of vegetative functions such as breathing and digesting; this he distinguished from peripheral sensory motor behavior, which can be more easily affected and changed.

From 1918 to 1933 Reich functioned in the mainstream of Viennese analysts. After 1933, he was preoccupied with researching bio-electrical energy sources, especially in terms of units of energy which he called "bions" and "orgone energy," which he believed could be accumulated out of the atmosphere to increase one's vitality. His work was not respected by the scientific community, although it is still defended by some.[37] Similar efforts to find the origins of life energy are underway in modern chemistry.[38] He has been viewed both as a charlatan and as a martyr for the causes of scientific and sexual freedom.

Reich wrote extensively about social conditions and the generally neurotic social structures and repressive attitudes toward natural functions, which he considered responsible for what he referred to as the "emotional plague."

His definition of healthy functioning is easily misunderstood because he seems to define the capacity for orgasm as the sole criterion for good psychic health. But then he extends the definition of a healthy orgastic response to include other less easily defined factors, such as the capacity to sustain an intimate relationship with a single partner. At the same time, he does say that it is unrealistic to expect healthy people to commit themselves to long-term sexual relationships to one person, as in marriage. Malcolm Brown, a neo-Reichian therapist, has written:

> It is not at all a question of the sheer quantity of libidinal energy charge and discharge generated, but the quality and degree of communion and fusion of one's subjectivity of being with the core being of the other that defines depth of orgastic satisfaction.[39]

At times Reich seems to say this, but at other times, to my mind, he does not.

Reich has been criticized for being too literal in his views on the importance of the orgasm. He is also criticized for the authoritarian and messianic flavor of his presentations. Reich imagined that the "emotional plague" accounted for people's negative reaction toward him, but it may have been his arrogance that was provocative.

Nic Waal, Reich's pupil who welcomed him to Norway during

the Nazi regime, wrote that psychoanalysts began to exclude Reich when his *Character Analysis* was published in 1933:

> Some did not understand the technique of working through the actual resistance pattern, the "here and now." Others . . . said this was not psychoanalysis at all, since it did not follow the technique of free association but selected the material actively. This difference of opinion between Reich and the rest could have been worked on, if not solved, through scientific and objective discussion. It did not have to go as far as exclusion. But Reich had already started on the road from character analysis to vegetotherapy. This was long before psychosomatic medicine on a psychodynamic basis had developed. It was a departure from psychoanalysis, in which treatment it was, in fact, a horrible offense even to touch the patient. It was to break all basic rules, and basic thinking on transference. It seemed to seduce the patient. The decent opponents thought that this was a break with Freud and basic rules. The indecent ones pointed out that Reich was a sexologist, and they viciously implied that he was devastating professional ethics.[40]

It is interesting that Reich was accused by the Freudians of the same crime that Freud was accused of by the conservative physicians. However, body therapy as it exists today owes a great debt to Reich's fearlessness. Though he remains controversial, the increasing prominence of body therapies continues to gather momentum in support of his techniques. His followers seem to fall into two major groups, the neo-Reichians, who continue his style, and the bioenergeticists, who follow Reich's pupil, Alexander Lowen, whom I will discuss later.[41]

Carl Jung

Each of the pioneers described here stood out against the forces of collectivization; they exemplified Jung's concept of individuation, the becoming of what one is meant to be even if it necessitates breaking with established expectations and opinions.

Although Jung initially accepted Freud's theory of sexuality as central to the cause of emotional illness, by 1912 he had many misgivings, resulting in his well-known break with Freud. Jung demonstrated boldness in his outspoken acknowledgment of the power of the unconscious to balance ego attitudes. His deviation from the materialism of the psychoanalytic movement led to his being labeled as a mystic by his colleagues.

For Jung, libido was conceptualized as psychic energy, a life-force only partially sexual. He placed less importance on the conflict in neurosis between instincts and the restrictive demands of society, and more on the conflict between intrapsychic functions and complexes. He saw regression as not necessarily pathological, but as a way of discovering creative solutions through contact with the collective unconscious. Only if the regression persisted into infantile behavior, with no creative resources emerging, could it be called pathological.

Jung's technique was much less rigid than Freud's. He is said to have been innovative, unpredictable and flexible in treatment. He is reported to have treated an insomniac by singing a lullaby. Whitmont and Yoram Kaufman write:

> In Jung's consulting room people danced, sang, acted, mimed, played musical instruments, painted, modeled with clay, the procedures seemingly limited only by Jung's inventiveness and ingenuity.

> To Jung, one of the most important aspects of the therapeutic process was the encounter, during the analytic hours, with the numinosum, that is, the religious, not in the sense of traditional organized religion, associated with churches, temples, and synagogues, but with one's inner religion, one's own sense of the divine within oneself.[42]

Jung did not make a point of focusing on the body and has written very little about bodily expression. Yet his psychology has furnished a container in which his followers have been able to develop many facets and directions, including body therapy and dance movement. Whitmont and Kaufman have described how group therapy and family therapy flourished in Jung's approach:[43]

> [In family therapy] Jungian principles, the understanding of the dynamics of shadow, animus, and anima projection, of communication difficulties based upon the differences of psychological types, can serve as vital therapeutic tools.[44]

They also state that in the 1920s Jungians were doing breathing therapy and what would later be called sensitivity training.[45]

Some of the factors in Jung's approach that have made it so adaptable are these:

1. The concept of psychic energy occurring on a continuous basis from dense to light, comparable to the light-energy continuum from infrared to ultraviolet. For wholeness, the therapist must be concerned with all phenomena, from the dense end which corresponds to the most primordial, instinctual level of biology, to the least dense areas of pure spirit.[46]

2. The concept of typology determining a person's preferences for visual, auditory or kinesthetic experience. (Arnold Mindell includes proprioception as a fourth category; see below, page 101.) Jung's statement that in active imagination some found it easier to dance out contents from the unconscious, rather than image them visually or auditorially, opened the door for body therapy.[47]

3. The technique of active imagination. The value of making direct contact with the unconscious contents, and the anthropomorphizing of those contents to render them manageable to the conscious ego, as Jung recommended, was adapted by gestalt therapy (Perls) and psychosynthesis (Assagioli), Bernstein and others. Penny Bernstein states in her text on dance movement theory:

> Carl Jung's development of the techniques of "active imagination" affording the patient a vehicle for expressing unconscious material also paved the way for movement therapy. Jung believed that it is vital for the individual to contact and understand the symbolic information from the unconscious. Once personal material is stripped from the complexes, their archetypal core provides a means for individualization and the experience of Selfhood. He utilized dreams and artistic processes as direct avenues into understanding what was "meant to be" for the person. For this purpose, Jung had used dance either as direct expression or through the "dancing out of one's dreams."[48]

4. The concept of the contrasexual functions, anima and animus.[49] By pointing out that each person contains biological and psychic aspects of the opposite sex, both inherited and acquired,

which one may recognize and integrate, Jung created a vast area for exploration. This area lends itself to a number of body techniques and leads quite naturally into them. For example, an anima or animus figure as personification of the archetype is remarkably easier to contact and dramatize than the abstract notion of one's instinctual energies.

5. The concept of the psyche's search for balance, especially in the typology of personality. The necessity for including the feeling and sensation functions into one's lifestyle implies the essential role of body awareness. Bernstein notes that Jung's psychological typology "seems to clarify this phenomenon. . . . Different orientations seem to suit the utilization of different theoretical approaches [in dance therapy]."[50]

6. The concept of the transcendent function, which Jung saw as a manifestation of the energy that springs from the tension of opposites, appearing spontaneously in dreams and visions.[51] Joan Chodorow writes:

> Jung describes the ego as a complex datum which is constituted primarily of a general awareness of the body. With sufficient attention to the body experience, it is possible to simultaneously express the unconscious through movement while maintaining an equally strong ego position through ongoing awareness of the body's reality.
>
> Although the impulse to move may spring from a source in the unconscious, the body, which allows the impulse to manifest itself, remains firmly rooted in the fact of its own existence. The actual act of moving creates proprioceptive and kinesthetic feedback which serves to confront the unconscious with the body ego's reality. . . . Since the body has the capacity to simultaneously manifest both conscious and unconscious, it may be our most potent tool toward the transcendent function.[52]

7. Jung's openness to consider Eastern thought and symbolism, for instance mandala formations, Yin and Yang energies, and the concept of Kundalini and the chakras. This latter aspect of Hinduism finally was perceived by the collective body of psychotherapists to be of importance in the late 1960s.

8. His attention to the physiological concomitants of complexes. The Word Association Test, with its record of the effects of emotion

on pulse rate, breathing and electrical conductivity of the skin, was the key to Jung's understanding of how mind and body functioned as a unit. Arnold Mindell says:

> Biofeedback researchers today credit him with the discovery of what they call "skin talk." Although Jung's work is not noted for physical research, he hypothesized that there was a chemical toxin behind schizophrenia, theorized about the mind-body relationship, interpreted dreams physiologically, and studied the significance of Kundalini yoga.[53]

9. The concept of synchronicity as an alternative to causal connectedness to explain mind-body functions. Mindell discusses this in his book, *Dreambody:*

> Though Jung used synchronicity and the concept of the psychoid unconscious mainly in conjunction with parapsychological phenomena, modern Jungians such as Ziegler, Bach, Meier, Scott, Redfearn, and Lockhart have applied the concept of synchronicity to the relationship between spontaneously appearing symbols and organic disorders.[54]

10. And finally, Jung's insistence on the integration of body and spirit, a concept that actually recapitulates the first concept named, psychic energy. Nathan Schwartz-Salant has underlined it thus:

> *Only when* the spirit exists as a reality, when psychic reality is a phrase with *objective meaning*—stemming from a transformation of the psyche such that a felt center exists—then and only then does a descent into the body lead to transformation, and to the experience of the somatic unconscious. Any other kind of descent, such as through body exercises, leads only to temporary changes which must always be repeated, for the lack of the spirit to—as the alchemists would say—"kill and transform the bodies" [Paracelsus] leads not to transformation, and surely not to the reality Jung knew as the somatic unconscious.
>
> Thus Jung's psychology is not anti-body but rather a proper guide to body. And any way that does not recognize the autonomy of the spirit and the existence of the archetypal realm can only lead to a very concrete view of body, which misses the mystery of the fundamental identity of body and psyche.[55]

These ten points are some of the influences of Jung on body

therapy. His followers continue to explore new ways for his theories to express themselves. It is due, I believe, to the fundamental healthiness of his personality and his connection with his own archetypal sources, that his psychology continues to grow and develop—to individuate. Whitmont is an important spokesman for the nonverbal techniques as they reflect Jung's position:

> The verbal dimension by itself is decidedly not enough. The primitives intuited this and instituted rituals to enhance psychic phenomena. Analytical psychotherapy is also attempting to cope with this problem. To that effect various non-verbal techniques are being incorporated into traditional practice; groups and movement, sensitivity training, and rituals are being employed so that psychic facts can be experienced more deeply and hitherto locked doors may be thrust open.[56]

Therapists of Later Influence

In addition to the above analysts and their followers, three other therapists had some influence on body therapy by focusing strongly on whole-body reactions to the therapeutic situation, keeping the physiological response in the foreground.

Franz Alexander, a Chicago analyst and author of *Psychosomatic Medicine,* combined physiological and psychological perspectives. A Freudian, he disagreed with orthodox theory on the nature of sexuality and granted greater importance to cultural influences. Alexander categorized people into those who face emergency by sympathetic nervous system reaction and those who face emergency by parasympathetic reaction. The former are prone to high blood pressure, diabetes, rheumatoid arthritis, goiter and headaches; the latter are prone to ulcers, diarrhea, colitis and constipation. He pointed out that coronary disease was an occupational hazard for physicians, lawyers and executives, and that certain personalities are accident prone.[57]

Jacob Moreno, the father of psychodrama, first used it as a therapy with self-help groups of Spittelburg prostitutes, and later with Viennese children. For years he held group theater at Carnegie Hall, opening the stage to anyone who wanted to work in that way.

He founded psychodrama at St. Elizabeth's Hospital (where dance therapy also began) as a way of assisting one in enacting important life situations and roles in order to know and express oneself more clearly. He attempted to resolve infantile fixations by uncovering their origins in role play, as we have seen that Ferenczi and Jung also did.

Fritz Perls, analyzed by Reich during 1931–32, was hostile toward the "dangers of the couch." Perls felt that most psychotherapy, and particularly psychoanalysis, was too intellectual, ignoring the physical sensations of the individual. One of his sayings was that we must "lose our heads to come to our senses." In order to facilitate that, he used his own bodily reactions to feed information back to the patient about how the patient affected others. He focused on the patient's posture, small movements, expressions, and other noticeable physiological reactions to bring the person into the present, the "here and now," and out of talking in an insulated way about the past or future.

Although he never gave credit to Jung, Perls used active imagination to illuminate patients' conflicts, especially in large groups in which he placed the primary patient "on the hot seat" while directing them in conversation with inner figures. He popularized psychotherapy at Esalen (1964–69) and influenced many other therapists, including Moshe Feldenkrais and Ida Rolf (see the next section). His methods focused on getting the person into direct contact with his or her immediate phenomenological field of awareness, especially by attending to the kinesthetic and sense impressions occurring from moment to moment.

Although he did not become a Reichian, his work shows Reich's influence in its emphasis on connecting appropriate feelings with thoughts, focusing on psychosomatic language, and the therapeutic use of impasse or "breakdown" of defenses.[58]

The Contributions of Dance Movement

During World War Two and its aftermath, the need arose for pragmatic ways of treating large numbers of psychically disturbed people. Long-term methods like analysis retreated to the background and the "brief" therapies became more popular. While followers of the men mentioned in the previous section adapted their theories to short-term work and to groups, they were joined by those influenced by dance movement.

I will first discuss the influences from dance movement and then examine contemporary leaders in body therapy with the understanding that there is substantial overlap, especially among the analytically oriented movement therapists. Gerda Alexander (see below) has said that at dance conferences one could recognize the pupils of each teacher while everyone was still in the lobby, for each teacher had a unique style which the students imitated.[59]

Isadora Duncan was a pioneer in modern dance who broke out of the stylized molds that contained professional dancers until the twentieth century. Although an American, she found more enthusiastic audiences in Europe for her emotional style and performance in costumes based on Greek classical art. She was illustrative of a growing interest in dance and movement that was quite strong in the twenties. She opened the way for dance as a form of expressiveness, combining emotional impressionism and movement in a way that was spontaneously in the movement, not routinized.

Another kind of influence came from *Frederick Matthias Alexander,* an Australian actor who learned by long intensive self-study with mirrors that the position of his head and neck had an important effect on the quality of his voice and the flow of his movements. He taught and developed his methods of postural correction over many years in England and America. He noted that by teaching children to sit or stand for prolonged periods before they are physiologically ready, we teach faulty posture and inefficient mobilization. He corrected these faults by retraining, by guiding students toward greater awareness, aliveness and sensuousness, and away from anxiety-provoking attitudes.

One of Alexander's concepts concerned lengthening the spine, concentrating on "long openness of spinal centrality," and breathing up and down that openness; another was to free the neck of tension and keep the head forward and up. In the interests of propriety, Alexander did not touch students below the shoulder, but his current followers may manipulate the entire body in order to teach alignment. The Alexander Method is used with individuals or groups.

Rudolph Von Laban devised a system of observing and notating motion, Labananalysis, which describes how an individual moves. Laban was a theoretician and dancer who attempted to organize space and dynamics of movement. His system has been further developed by Irmgard Bartenieff, Marion North and Warren Lamb. One aspect of this system, called Effort/Shape, offers a tool for the study of unconscious and conscious processes. Joan Chodorow, a dance therapist and Jungian analyst, has explained this:

> Effort gives us a way of looking at a person's intentional attitudes toward *Time . . . Shape . . . Weight . . .* and *Flow* of muscular tension. Depending on the way we combine these elements, the movement experience may strengthen our connection to the objective external world, or it may relate us to our more subjective inner world. . . .
>
> Effort/Shape is one component of Labananalysis which also includes Space Harmony and the Movement Fundamentals developed by Bartenieff. As Effort/Shape depicts the quality of Movement, Space Harmony deals with the body's relationship to itself. Just as Jung has given us a psychology which encompasses the vastness of our potential, Laban's work offers us a movement-based model for human wholeness. Each presents a framework through which we may study the same ultimate reality.[60]

Moshe Feldenkrais, like Frederick Alexander, was technically not a dancer, but is included here because he evolved a technique of exercises designed to improve alignment, posture and, ultimately, awareness. He has created over a thousand body-mind movement sequences aimed at greater flexibility and coordination, and more efficient development of the body's energy. Feldenkrais wrote:

> Awareness is the highest stage in man's development, and when it is complete it maintains a harmonious "rule" over the body's activities. When an individual is strong, so are his passions, and his ability and vitality are on the same scale. It is impossible to suppress these prime movers without reducing his total potential. The

improvement of awareness is preferable to any attempt to overcome instinctive drives. For the more nearly complete a man's awareness becomes, the more he will be able to satisfy his passions without infringing on the supremacy of awareness. And every action will become more human.[61]

This Israeli teacher has a large international following and a reputation for dealing successfully with a wide variety of problems.

Three American women have been prominent in the recognition of dance as a valuable form of therapy.

Mary Starks Whitehouse, a European-trained American dancer, says about herself, "I turned into a dance therapist without realizing it, simply because no such thing existed when I started."[62] She describes the transition period in the fifties when she became the analysand of a personal patient of Jung, and saw that she could enlarge the meaning of her art by using it to work with people in a way that opened them to being whole persons. Her style focuses on experiencing polarities that are inherently present in the pattern of movement, on active imagination, and on helping the client to find his or her "authentic movement." She sees movement as a revelation of the Self, which in Jung's view is the regulating center of the psyche.

Marian Chace began to use dance as therapy in her own dance studio, but the major expansion of her ideas took shape during her work at St. Elizabeth's Hospital in Washington, D.C., with psychotic patients in the forties and fifties, before transquilizers were developed. Her most basic concept is that dance is communication and fulfills a basic human need. Her aim was to communicate with patients by moving with them. "Both the psychotic patient and the dancer make use of symbolic body action to communicate emotions and ideas that defy everyday use of language."[63]

Chace used rhythm as an ordering principle, and the circle as a container and means of closure. She studied and characterized the action patterns of different diagnostic categories. She was talented at contacting withdrawn patients and evoking their life-force, bringing them into the present with her.

Trudi Schoop, a Swiss dancer, improvised her approach to dance therapy while working in a mental hospital in California. Her concepts about working with patients were developed by trial and error out of her own experience. Her goal is to help patients attain a greater degree of integration, of wholeness, as we move through life experiencing two levels of existence simultaneously: the UR, meaning transcendental experience, and the human, earthbound existence. She stresses that fusion of mind and body occurs by their recognized interaction.[64]

Gerda Alexander is a Danish dancer who, like F.M. Alexander (no relation), came to understand more about the body by observing her own infirmity, which developed after years of dancing. She devised a method called Eutony (harmonious tonus), which aims at a state of physical and psychic tension which permits optimal functioning in the human organism considered as a whole. It consists of first identifying any tension affecting the organism and manifesting itself in posture, movement, breathing, voice, etc. With the help of tests, the eutonist explores and undertakes to correct the body's problem areas.

Gerda Alexander, like Reich, presumes that traumatizing affective experience contributes to the formation of rigid, autonomous zones. Marcel Gaumond, a Canadian analyst, has noted that this corresponds to Jung's view that complexes always have a physical component.[65] However Gerda Alexander does not see these rigidities as only the results of purely sexually blocked energy or traumatic emotional experiences. Like F.M. Alexander and Feldenkrais, she feels that chronic tension is often the result of erroneous or inadequate attitudes toward the body.

Eutony teaches that each person has a unique destiny which no one can know entirely. This basic attitude causes the eutonist to refrain from any sort of suggestion, other than to observe what is being experienced. There is no attempt to force the liberation of emotion or sexuality, though it is expected that liberation will unfold with the increase of conscious perceptions of the body. Gerda Alexander's goals are mastery of tonal flexibility; adaptable breathing; economic movement characterized by lightness of execution and maximal results attained by minimal effort; awareness of touch and contact; and the furthering of individuation through growth in body-awareness. She has described her approach:

> From my first contact with Jung's ideas in 1929, I have felt Jung's approach much nearer to the experiences of Eutony than that of any group of the Freudian school. In Eutony, the individuation process is based on the great importance of one's own body for the development of the total person.
>
> Already in its early prenatal state, the child is influenced by the vital, emotional, and spiritual state of its mother, by the sound of its parents' voices and especially by music. The development of the awareness of body sensations in skin tissues, muscles, and bone structure seems to awaken impressions from the prenatal state: vague feelings of comfort and satisfaction, sadness or anxiousness come up and are passed through. These states cannot be reached through verbal analysis, as can impressions from later periods. Generally they present themselves with extraordinary clearness of the entire situation: surroundings, smells, sounds, colors, and emotions, often combined with a sudden clear understanding: There is the reason for any wrong reactions.[66]

Eutony distinguishes between *touch,* through which we live our external bodily form, remaining within the periphery of our skin, and *contact,* which allows us to press beyond the awareness of touch.

Gaumond has written about the possibilities for reciprocity between Eutony and analysis, regarding them as distinct yet complementary processes:

> In Eutony, the pupil has the opportunity of coming face-to-face with the unconscious contents of his physical world and can then turn to analysis for clarification of the psychic contents often brought to the surface during the encounter.[67]

Contemporary Body Therapists

In contemporary psychotherapy a number of styles of body therapy have been developing out of the influential styles of the pioneers and dancers described above.

The major locations for Reichian work and training are Denmark, London and the Asssociation for Orgonomy in New York. Alexander Lowen broke from the New York Reichian group and founded, with John Perriakos, the Institute of Bioenergetic Analysis in New York. Bioenergetics is also a major influence in California, for example at the Eastern Growth Center at Big Sur, and the Center for Energetic Studies at Berkeley under the leadership of Stanley Keleman.

Ilana Rubenfeld is a New York therapist who combines the methods of F.M. Alexander and Feldenkrais with gestalt therapy. Her approach, called the Rubenfeld Synergy Method, is described by Anita Greene:

> The two methods [body-mind work and gestalt therapy] emphasize inner kinesthetic awareness of how one habitually acts and a non-judgmental attitude toward whatever happens—both are prerequisites for change. Both aim toward reeducation of the nervous system, especially the motor cortex.[68]

Biochemist *Ida Rolf* developed the approach of Structural Integration. This involves deep massage designed to loosen the fascia systemically throughout the body in ten separate sessions. Rolf believes that fascia (the connective tissue that holds the body together and envelopes the muscles and internal organs) is a primary mechanism for retaining memory traces of early experiences. By loosening this tissue early memories are released and body alignment improves. Rolf, a student of Perls, feels it is important to be able to reexperience early trauma to the psyche-body. Verbalizing about the trauma or other early experiences is encouraged by Rolfers (those who have learned this treatment), but it is not their primary focus, nor is the work of analyzing and integrating the psychic material that emerges.

Arthur Janov's Primal Therapy requires that patients commit themselves to three weeks of residential treatment at Janov's clinic in Los Angeles. During this time the patient submits to emotional and physical deprivation in order to reach the deepest level of psychic pain which she or he then expresses in screaming, considered by Janov to be the most valid level of release from frozen tension.

Though Janov's methods derive from Reich and Perls, many therapists consider his theory simplistic, ignoring the importance of muscular armoring and transference.

Anita Greene is a New York Jungian analyst who combines analysis with body therapy. She studied with Ilana Rubenfeld. Greene's method is to elicit and encourage the expression of contents of complexes, through attention to breathing, direct touch and massage.[69]

Joan Chodorow is a Jungian analyst and dance therapist in Los Angeles. Her work is influenced by Trudi Schoop and Mary Whitehouse. Chodorow asks the patient to move in accordance with the feelings that arise in the session, then move through feelings associated with opposite attitudes. This is one way in which she seeks to promote the differentiation and integration of inner experiences.[70]

Personal Influences

I would like to describe in more detail the work of some body therapists which I have personally experienced. They are Alexander Lowen, bioenergeticist; Malcolm Brown, neo-Reichian; Albert Pesso, psychomotor psychotherapist; Arnold Mindell, Jungian analyst; Carolyn Grant Fay, Jungian dance therapist. These five have directly influenced my own work. In addition, I include Edward Whitmont and Marion Woodman, Jungian analysts; though I have had no direct contact with their work, both have been prominent in my experience because of their clarifying writing on the subject.

Alexander Lowen, trained by Wilhelm Reich, has written many books describing his theory and work. He differs from Reich in that Lowen does not feel bound to attack the muscular armoring ring by ring in Reich's prescribed order, but determines his approach according to the diagnostic information given by the patient's body and psychic functioning. He also makes less use of direct body techniques and more use of exercise, stress positions and verbal emotional release techniques.

Lowen's office furnishings consist of a bed, a chair, a basin and a stool. He usually begins a session with breathing exercises, but with the patient standing, partially clothed, or stretched backward over the stool rather than lying down. Energy is mobilized by stress positions and exercises, and he then does deep pressure and massage in blocked areas.

My experience of the bioenergetic therapy sessions was that the therapist was very aggressive and directive, and there was little opportunity during the session for introspection. The exploration of one's own inner response to the work was expected to take place after the session. This appreciation of Lowen is by body therapist Malcolm Brown:

> We who work in the field of body psychotherapy are all deeply indebted to Lowen and his spirit of rebellion because he has done us the considerable service of breaking away from the more objectionable one-sidedness of the orthodox Reichian position without rejecting its positive virtues and strengths. For instance, he has not ignored the cerebral cortex and Central Nervous System and idolized the Autonomic Nervous System as Reich has done. On the contrary, he has formulated a theory of optional energy development in the healthy person which gives an evenly balanced emphasis to both nervous networks, claiming that both the cortex and the genitals each function as the two basic condensers of energy charges within the organism and that both play an indispensable role as energy mobilizers whenever the subject has to confront difficult tasks and challenging reality solutions.[71]

Patients are constantly encouraged to increase their tolerance of the stress positions and exercises in the belief that the more alive and less armored their energy flow, the stronger their condenserlike qualities for energy charge and discharge in their bodies—hence the greater excitement and enjoyment of life they can tolerate. Lowen has published extensively on the essential concepts of body language and bioenergetic body therapy.

Bioenergetics has been criticized for its tendency to equate vitality with gross physical activity, while ignoring the kind of deep spiritual vitality which is not visible to the observer. In fact, this could be a possible criticism of most of the body therapies.

Malcolm Brown, a neo-Reichian, now lives and practices primarily in Italy with his wife Katherine Ennis, but does occasional training workshops in the United States. He was the patient of Ola Raknes, a Norwegian trained by Reich when Raknes and Brown were both living in London in the sixties. Brown is significantly influenced by Jung, and is critical of most other body therapists because he feels they are not sufficiently cognizant of spiritual values occurring in self-actualized persons.

Brown has described his and his wife's work as follows:

> Our body-centered energy-mobilization techniques are for us exclusively intermediary in function, and never ends in themselves. They mediate the opening of the client's awareness to his own neglected soul-powers and intuitive capacities for self-evolution and self-fulfillment.
>
> By placing our four hands on those parts of the patient's body that are most likely to produce a widespread simultaneous dispersion of energy flow into distant parts of the metabolism, we stand a good chance of softly challenging the ego-defense network without over-threatening and provoking it to assume a position of defended vigilance. Sometimes this is best accomplished by touching the most tense muscles or regions of the body in a soft, immobile nurturing mode for as long as fifteen minutes. At other times it is best accomplished by touching the least tense parts in a three-phase mobile style, which begins with a purely nurturing mode of touch and gradually converts over to a low-grade catalytic mode invoking movement and pressure and then returns to an immobile, purely nuturing mode.[72]

Malcolm Brown came eventually to reject the goal-directed charging up and discharging of great quantities of energy in favor of holding and pressure. He says, "Such energetic catharsis must happen spontaneously from within to be of healing value, and even then the most which is accomplished adds up to nothing more than a very brief jolting and shaking up of the intact muscular armoring."[73] He works toward "the quiet awakening of the core longitudinal energy currents and the spontaneous unfolding of the repressed, and later the collective and personal unconscious networks and their accompanying repressed core soul powers of intuition."[74]

Brown's schema for reading the body is as follows:

1. *Back*

a. Upper-half: Seat of aggressive tendencies which predispose the individual to keep an optional separation between self and the other person toward whom they are sympathetically drawn by the feeling flow in the breast.

b. Lower-half: Seat of self-assurance and passionate tendencies.

2. *Front*

a. Upper-half: Sympathetic feeling centers on affection and love.

b. Lower-half: Vital feeling center ensuring stability, ongoing unity, equilibrium and self-contentment.

Brown's technique includes mobilization of energy exercises to be done individually; exercises in pairs to promote "horizontal grounding" and "vertical grounding," which focus on submissive and assertive energies respectively; and direct touch by the therapists. He considers "creatively disintegrative regression" necessary to the healing process.

> The challenge to all psychotherapy is to transform the regulative system of the body away from the dominance of the corticocerebrospinal circuits and toward the Self-regulative creative unconscious in vital centers below the cerebral cortex.[75]

(This is the corrective process to the circumstances described above by Halliday, wherein life is subjected to conditioning which promotes bodily disorders instead of being allowed to unfold naturally.)

According to Brown, there are four stages of dearmoring:

1) Primaling—undoing stasis by charge/discharge, which is autocentric.

2) Identification and ownership of unsatisfied primary feeling needs from the past, starting with the mother-child relationship during the first year of life.

3) Confrontation with the shadow, the negative-archetypal instinctual needs in the body.

4) Confrontation with one's sexuality.

Albert Pesso and his wife, Diane, discovered and developed a method of psychotherapy and emotional reeducation called Pesso System Psychomotor Therapy. This method involves creating a setting and structure in group sessions for people to correct negative early experience and to create new patterns and solutions through discharging emotions and role-playing.

First the patient is encouraged to identify feelings, then give action to them, then recognize the object of the feelings, and finally convey this to the appropriate person in role-play. In order to clarify and simplify the experience, a group member is designated to portray the negative aspects of the object, and another to play the ideal object. The subject comes to see how it would be to have a different outcome for his or her feelings. The goal is to be in touch with one's potential, not in an intellectual way, but experientially, supported by the safety of the group.

In relating to the "ideal object" in this supportive and suggestive setting, the patient often reaches an archetypal connection. Pesso, like Brown, is significantly influenced by Jung. His psychodrama usually reaches a profound level wherein there is a ritualistic quality. For example, a patient suffering from memory of oral deprivation has an opportunity not only to experience asking for and receiving the breast of the Good Mother (in symbolic role-play), but also to experience an infusion of life-energy from the Great Mother.

Pesso sees symptoms as energy and, in themselves, the beginnings of the cure:

> Our bodies are endlessly and immediately reacting to everything that we really feel. Our body is a source of truth. Our soul speaks to us through our body. And all those symptoms inside are the energy of what we can become . . . the seed of the unborn self.[76]

Pesso has an extensive workshop training program and a course leading to certification as an Adjunct Psychomotor Therapist.

Arnold Mindell, a Jungian analyst in Switzerland, considers pain and illness to be signposts from the unconscious speaking in the language of the body. His principal focus is to encourage the amplification and expression of the body's involuntary signals in order to translate those signals into healing images. Body work, he writes in *Dreambody,* extends the experiential dimension of dreams and generally increases the possibility for knowing the unconscious. On the other hand, dream work gives body processes a personalized, visual structure which—as far as I know—they have never had before in therapeutic work.[77]

He sees individuation as a state in which "the eyes, skin color, lips, hand motions, body posture, voice tone, words and fantasies all manifest one and the same piece of information, the real personality, a living myth."[78]

Mindell's "dreambody," a reformulation of the concept of the "subtle body," occupies the space between body and psyche. He explains the concept in this way:

> When the dreambody manifests itself as an energetic charge shooting through the spine, we could call it by its ancient name, the Kundalini. When it is experienced as the essence of life, it is Mercury. When one visualizes its energy as streaming through the body, it is the twelve meridian system. If one sees it and acts on this vision we have Gestalt identification. If one feels it as a cramp in breathing, it is called character armor. If one senses it and changes, we might speak of biofeedback. If it appears as a force pushing one in the stomach to do a new task, it is personal power. Obviously, we need a unified approach to the body.
>
> Psychologists with sufficient training and flexibility to follow individual dreambody processes will discover that terms such as analysis, psychotherapy and body work must expand to the point where psychology allows the human being to touch upon every known theory and practice. Dreambody process may begin to "talk" in the style of Gestalt, psychodrama, or active imagination or it may ask to be "Rolfed" with a penetrating massage. At other times or in other cases, the body may begin to spontaneously enact unknown postures such as Hatha Yoga's asanas or enter into deep states of meditation characteristic of Zen. Balancing movements of the head characteristic of the Alexander technique also occur. Sometimes the body asks for a shaking typical of bioenergetic exercises; other times its spirit slips into a shamanistic dance. This spectrum of behavior is important for anyone interested in physiology. The Western therapist, in the face of the body work spectrum, needs to understand and accept forms of psyche and physical behavior that would be completely normal for a yogi, shaman or acupuncture specialist.
>
> Understanding and accepting the dreambody as process, however,

requires factual knowledge about its behavior and the courage to go to one's own limits in order to let the dreambody come into awareness. For the dreambody itself hovers between body sensation and mythical visualization.[79]

Carolyn Grant Fay, a dance therapist who heads the School for the Expressive Arts of the C.G. Jung Educational Center in Houston, studied with Mary Starks Whitehouse. She incorporates Jungian principles into her individual and group dance therapy work.

It was largely Fay's influence that led me to become an analyst, through experiencing analytical psychology in dance. She often works with groups by setting an archetypal theme with words and music, and allowing people to create their own individual movement in association to the theme. Individually she works by having one talk about oneself and one's current mood or situation, and then waiting till the body is moved to express itself. She sometimes combines art with the music and dance, and verbal processing always consolidates the psychic content.

Marion Woodman, a Zurich-trained Jungian analyst in Toronto, Ontario, uses a group program to contain the body work in workshop sessions that last from September to June. The program is divided into four units, each consisting of eight sessions, two hours each, once a week: 1) Body and dream work; 2) Evolutionary movement; 3) Voice; 4) Masks.

Each session begins with deep relaxation and meditation on patients' dream symbols. Woodman says, "Every session someone goes into preverbal material and I do as much holding as necessary. A trained body person carries on with the class."[80] The major emphasis is on breath. All kinds of music, and silence, are used in the groups. Almost all sessions end with free dance. Body work is used with all patients who will allow it, and most patients choose to have it, sometimes in the analytic sessions, sometimes in the workshop. Courses vary according to needs.

Woodman is best known for her insightful writing and analytic work with individuals suffering from eating disorders.[81]

Edward C. Whitmont, once a patient of Jung, has been a vocal proponent of the incorporation of nonverbal techniques into Jungian analysis. In addition to group and family therapy, he has described and defended the use of body-awareness techniques to amplify dreams and intensify affect, and contact preverbal contents. He has explained his use of enactment in analysis:

> Enactment is an adaptation of Gestalt and psychodrama methods to the Jungian process. But it also includes nonverbal pantomiming, which often comes closer to the expression of preverbal affect than standard Gestalt and psychodrama techniques do. In contradistinction to Perls and Moreno, who intended to address themselves primarily, if not exclusively to the experiencing of the immediate here-and-now and hence rejected interpretation, I do not hesitate to use interpretation after, but not before, the experiential working through. Interpretation as well as active or guided imagination, may frequently be helpful and even essential in amplifying the affect experience and integrating it into the overall pattern of the transformation process and of meaning. . . . As a method in itself it [enactment] is not adequate to replace the analytic process, as Perls, who was unfamiliar with Jung's works, thought.[82]

Whitmont practices in New York and incorporates enactment and a variety of expressive techniques into individual analysis. He also combines analysis with group and family therapy, and perhaps can be said to represent the epitome of the Americanization of analytical psychology.

These people have influenced me in that I have experienced each of them as profoundly effective with what they do. In my own development as a body therapist I experience myself as drawing on my contact with these approaches in an eclectic style. I am grateful to all these people whose input I am aware of as I work with patients.

3

Integrating Body Therapy and Depth Psychology

Introduction

Respect for the power and the dynamic transforming quality of the unconscious is the essence of the Jungian tradition. Jung's understanding of the complexes and their resistance to conscious manipulation led to the development of a treatment form in which the contents of complexes are allowed to emerge into consciousness in a manner consistent with a person's individuation process.[83] This means that the analyst attempts to create a safe environment in which the individuation process can unfold, rather than forcing adaptation in the patient by directive methods.

However, a wide diversity of opinion exists as to what constitutes directiveness, confrontation, amplification and interpretation. There are serious questions about what interventions by the analyst are called for and when they are appropriate.

Reading the literature of recent years, it is obvious that analysts are not bound by the traditional dialectical model, which, as Nathan Schwartz-Salant points out, is only *one* of Jung's models for the analytical relationship.[84] Many factors complicate this issue, such as whether the phase of work and nature of the transference will allow a given intervention, and whether an intervention is appropriate for a particular type of patient or diagnostic configuration.

In recent years the field of psychotherapy has gained considerably in its awareness of the nature and treatment of personality disorders, and in the awareness of transference-countertransference phenomena; but there remains much confusion about the nature of the healing process, the question of when to intervene and the use of verbal or nonverbal techniques.

Some analysts resolve the questions by emphasizing the need for great consistency in setting the frame and following a carefully thought-out procedure. Others focus on the importance of remaining flexible in the analytical relationship. Certainly, as analyst Harriet

Machtiger puts it, "The issue of what is therapeutically useful is enormously important, complicated, and controversial.[85]

In view of this already existing uncertainty and questioning of methodology, does the analyst dare to physically touch the patient, thus throwing another dynamically loaded issue (body contact) into the vessel?

The fact is, given the current trend of openness to the body among analysts, it may be expected that body therapy will be more and more incorporated into analysis. The focus then will be on theoretically and practically integrating verbal and nonverbal techniques.

Some resistance on the part of analysts to incorporating touch techniques is understandable and valid. For one thing, as noted earlier, it reflects the collective resistance to the emergence of the feminine in the objective psyche (collective unconscious). Our patriarchal culture, which strives to conquer nature, is experiencing an upheaval from the long-suppressed instinctual values; that upheaval, as seen in the previous chapter, has been conceptualized as the "return of the goddess." Overvaluing the rational and ignoring the body has resulted in fear of being overwhelmed by the eruption of desire if we relax our guard; the other danger is that we can fall into the opposite extreme and allow the needs of the body to take precedence over less tangible values, perhaps even block the process of individuation by creating a "slave to the instincts" mentality. As our culture struggles to find balance in this issue, so we as individuals struggle to know how to manage our bodies and the embodied complexes of our patients. However, the emergence has begun and cannot be turned back, hence the questions raised by body therapy must be responsibly addressed.

Other resistances to doing body therapy involve both theoretical and practical issues. Some of my own resistances, which I believe are typical among analysts, are as follows:

1. I am afraid of using a body technique if I think I may be interfering with the patient's process. Often it is not clear whether an intervention will divert the patient's own process or amplify it in a constructive way. When I am not clear, I usually opt not to act, to wait.

2. I am afraid that the content of the body therapy will obscure or interfere with the transference. If I intervene with a body technique, I could be seen by some patients as acting out the parental role, even though my intention is to explore and not to gratify.

3. The timing of an intervention is crucial. In using as active an intervention as a body technique, I sometimes encounter inertia in myself. That is, I don't *want* to get up and move. It may be that I am responding to something about the patient's timing that is valid, or it may be that I am reluctant to expose myself at that time for some personal reason. Sometimes these differences are not clear, and I can only act on intuition as to whether to push against my resistance or not.

4. Sometimes I tell myself I don't know enough about this person's body to use an intervention. To some extent that is always true, but therapists must come to trust the communication, conscious and unconscious, with the patient in order to act with conviction.

5. I often tell myself I don't know enough about anatomy and physiology to use a body intervention. To some extent this also will always be true. We cannot guarantee that we will never make a mistake and cause physical or psychic harm to a patient who trusts us (nor can we in verbal analysis). This anxiety can move me to continue studying the human body or it can paralyze me as a body therapist.

6. I wonder if I can ever feel comfortable as a body therapist since I don't have a strong sensation function (see section below on typology). Of all the body therapies, dance movement seems to be the most natural method for me; still, I have some inhibitions about the assertiveness it requires.

These questions and inhibitions come and go as I work. They are not uncommon and indeed may even be healthy. To be absolutely sure of oneself and one's work is simply a sign of inflation.

In the following sections I will put forth some of the issues facing analysts and other depth psychologists regarding gratification, transference, typology, and training in the use of body therapy, particularly the use of touch. As I am still an early explorer in this area, I am writing to help clarify the questions and perhaps shed light on the resistances generally felt toward working with the body. Only if these resistances are made conscious can they be overcome and a more useful frame of reference developed, one which will aid the overcoming of the mind-body split in analysis and in the culture.

Touch and the Analytic Model

Before discussing the question of touch in analysis, several related issues must be separated out. Just as physicists have learned that they cannot collect data without influencing what is observed, so analysts can no longer presume to intervene innocuously on any level with the patient. The myth of the "innocent observer-interpreter" is no longer acceptable. Today's analyst must recognize the reciprocity between the analyst's and the patient's psychic systems.

The importance of monitoring one's interventions by carefully noting the patient's subsequent associations and behavior has been stressed by William Goodheart, who believes that seemingly minor infractions of the "analytic frame" are received unconsciously by the patient as invasions or denigrations.[86] Some traditional analysts consider that even asking the patient about dreams, or offering interpretations and amplifications of dreams, is an intrusive, non-therapeutic intervention, much less approaching the person in a sociable or physical way.[87]

Opinions differ on whether and how an analyst may touch a patient, depending on the analyst's theoretical model of the analytic relationship. Goodheart takes a very firm stance against abandoning the symbolic-analytic approach, and challenges the rationale that the therapist must sometimes abandon the symbolic in order to strengthen the ego in some patients before proceeding with analysis:

> This attitude leads some therapists into offering general intellectuali-
> zations, such as inferences about intrapsychic, psychological,
> dynamic, and archetypal processes or into the giving of advice, the
> sharing of personal experiences, the sharing of objects, the touching
> of the patient physically, the hugging of the patient, and, in some
> instance, even into making love to the patient. . . .
>
> I contend that it is the therapist's *not* abandoning the analytic
> attitude which strengthens the patient's ego and experience of self,

which aids the patient's capacity to hold himself or herself to a symbolic and reflecting attitude toward unconscious experiences in spite of what pressures there might be to do otherwise. . . . We signal to the patient that we know he or she has a Self hidden within, which will and can join us in this enterprise.[88]

At the same time other Jungians appear to be operating under different models. Mindell encourages the patient to amplify his or her body language and analyze it like a dream.[89] Whitmont also considers body techniques as an expansion or amplification of active or guided meditation, embracing not merely the eidetic (vivid images) but the proprioceptive (stimuli in the body).[90] Florence Wiedemann writes that with women patients in certain stages of animus development she acts deliberately on the countertransference stages of mother, father, teacher and sister;

I use the idealizing transference in the same way good-enough mothers do, to socialize their children. . . . If she does not perform and relate to the world, the consequence is my displeasure.[91]

The analyst's role is to help the patient develop sufficient ego strength for living an adult life, to help her take steps toward becoming competent in the pursuits of her life, to encourage her to take the next necessary steps, and to discourage her passive-aggressive behavior by confronting it directly.[92]

And Woodman, as noted above, says she does "as much holding as necessary" in her movement groups when someone regresses into preverbal material.[93]

Clearly there are a variety of models of analytical style within the framework of Jungian psychotherapy. (These are discussed at length in Andrew Samuels's book, *Jung and the Post-Jungians.)*

Goodheart proposes three interactional fields which operate between analyst and patient (corresponding to a similar schema arrived at by Harold Searles and Robert Langs): persona-restoring field, complex-discharging field and secured-symbolizing field. According to Goodheart the analyst and patient operate in any one of these fields at any given time; one field will dominate the interaction and determine its characteristics.[94]

With the correct analytic attitude, writes Goodheart, the persona-restoring and complex-discharging fields resolve and the secured-symbolizing field can be sustained; then free mutual exploration of fantasy and reality through the use of symbols can occur. He warns that the analyst can be mistaken in identifying the field, rendering analytical interventions useless, at best. Goodheart describes the situation when the secured-symbolizing field is firm:

> In these deeper areas, the use of painting, drawing, journals, sandplay and other non-verbal manifestations of the transcendent function as described by Jung and his followers all have their place, as may personal revelations, direct responses to the patient, answering of questions and the like. If the field is truly secure, the analyst follows his own individuation and that of the patient with some assuredness that his behavior will not represent complex-discharges or persona-restorations.[95]

He goes on to warn that many interventions perceived by the analyst to come from his or her individuating response, actually are complex-discharging.

> Finally, I believe it is important to observe that these practical propositions apply to every analyst-patient interaction, regardless of the diagnosis of the patient, of the genetic, dynamic, or developmental background, of whether the meetings occur once or five times a week, and of whether the patient sits in a chair or lies on a couch. The propositions seem to me to be fundamentals that are universally present whenever analysis takes places between two people.[96]

Schwartz-Salant also describes a schema of different stages in treatment, specifically in treating narcissistic problems. Stage One involves working through idealizing and mirroring transferences, "during which the importance of introversion, imagination, and the healing function of the archetype is established."[97] Stage Two is characterized by "the emergence of the split-off Self that has a largely feminine and Dionysian character."[98]

These theorists propose that the appropriateness of specific analytical intervention changes during different stages of analysis. I believe this to be true. The major question about the use of touch and other forms of body therapy, therefore, is whether they are appropriate interventions when a complex has been constellated. In the following example of the use of body therapy in a Jungian analysis, I will describe the conditions that led me to revise the analytic model that I began with in order to include physical interventions at this point in our work.

Lee, a woman in her mid-forties, had been in analysis with me for almost two years. She had worked well in recording and reflecting upon her dreams, and had come through a period of deep depression to being able to do some creative writing which excited and fulfilled her. Her relationship with her husband and children had improved, and she had made important decisions concerning a career. However, it seemed significant that she had never shown any very intense emotion during her sessions. Emotions were expressed symbolically, but not embodied. Her body was well insulated, overweight and undercharged. She did not enjoy any physical activity, including sexual play, and often ignored her body's messages by overeating when she was not hungry. She also had high blood pressure.

She was not terribly concerned about these characteristics, adopting an attitude of, "That's just the way I am," but many dreams repeated the image of hidden fire in the house. Such dreams signify a dangerous condition, often being precursors of illness or accidents. Then a dream appeared about a little girl, hidden and imprisoned in a secret part of the house "behind the fireplace." I proposed the possibility of our working directly with the body in an exploratory way. She had been in one of my dance movement workshops, and while she enjoyed the experience she did not feel that it had touched her in any profound way. Unlike some participants, she experienced no strong emotions, only a general feeling of pleasure and well-being in being able to move without embarrassment and with a sense of freedom and lack of self-consciousness. Soon after, she had powerful imagery related to the workshop; dreams indicated that a very strong masculine energy had been constellated and was moving in her.

Up until now I had worked in a rather conservative analytic style with Lee. Most of the time was spent associating to and amplifying dream images, relating them to her waking life, her behavior, her attitudes toward significant people, to me, to early relationships with parents. She had shifted from a decidedly negative mother and idealized father to more complete parental images, but never demonstrated much affect in sessions. She saw me as a respected "guide" whom she was careful not to impose on. She admitted her need to protect me, and became able to see how she identified with the all-giving mother which she acted out in many areas of her life.

The introduction of body therapy into our work would represent a drastic change, and I wondered how that would manifest itself in transference-countertransference issues. She was slowly coming into more contact with her own needs and her capacity to make some demands on the environment. My expectation was that direct body touch would enhance that process, open her more to feeling responses by contacting energy that could not be reached by verbal methods because of her long-standing insulation against passion.

I approached the work from this framework: I intended to use breathing and exercise to mobilize energy and to use direct touch to focus the energy in specific body areas where energy seemed to be contained or pent-up. This basically Reichian model of dearmoring was not intended to be gratifying, but to explore and amplify responsivity to physical and psychic stimuli.

My decision to change styles to include nonverbal work and direct touch was not without conflict. On one hand I saw that the patient was working well and making significant changes in herself and her life. Possibly the dreams of fire might have led to bodily changes in the course of conventional analysis. Perhaps I was pushing her, directing her unconscious, by suggesting body therapy; possibly I would cause her to distrust me, to see me as her intrusive mother, not respecting her individual journey, her need to remain physically insulated. On the other hand, I saw her hypertension and overeating as serious symptoms of unrelatedness to the body which warranted at least a try at intervention. In the dreams of the imprisoned child, the child was not able to ask for help. The dream-ego of the patient heard the child's cries, but was not able to convince her to come forward and be liberated. I saw body therapy as a stronger impetus, another tool like dream work and active imagination with which to communicate with the imprisoned child.

The ambivalence of Lee toward her first body therapy session would be seen in the following session, when she reported that she felt more aware, less tense and generally relaxed, but had had a dream about being taken captive by black intruders, and defended herself with a long knife. Her friend, who was also captured, got undressed and got into the bathtub, which the dreamer felt made her too vulnerable. Consciously she had had a good response, but in the unconscious she experienced a conflict. To some extent she was willing to disclose herself and enter the transforming vessel or tub, but she also felt vulnerable and mobilized against dangerous aspects of the shadow which threatened to overwhelm her. This resistance had to be acknowledged and understood in terms of her ego strength and the capacity of her body to handle the release of new levels of energy without discomfort.

The Meaning of Touch

What do we know about the use of touch in analysis? For one thing, we know that so much can be read into a simple touch that an analyst needs to penetrate his or her own need to make the intervention as well as to predict how it will be received, regardless of the casualness or profundity of the touch.

Here are some possible motives for touching the patient: amplification and exploration of unconscious contents; mirroring; dearmoring; gratification of the patient's needs for contact, affection, containment, parenting and sexuality; and gratification of the therapist's need for the same things. The line between these kinds of touch is sometimes thin or diffused because of the relative lack of body awareness in our culture. Consequently, it may be valuable to examine these motives for touch in greater detail.

1. *Exploration and Amplification.* Most instances of enactment, positioning, assisting the patient in moving or feeling a body part, and encouragement to pay attention to some bodily state occurs here. Probably much of the kind of touching described by Mindell, Gerda Alexander, F.M. Alexander, Feldenkrais, Whitmont and dance therapists is in this category.

2. *Mirroring.* This occurs at times when the patient needs the therapist or another patient to join in a bodily experience, such as

pushing or pulling against, dancing with or screaming with. Many people have never had their assertiveness mirrored or supported in any way by another. Also, such an experience can be valuable in breaking out of a pattern of alienation, especially when the alienation is largely archetypal and not part of a neurotic withholding. Joan Chodorow describes an example in which the archetype of the wounded healer was activated:

> Watching her, the therapist notices that her own body is becoming tense with restricted, shallow breathing. In Anna's pain, she recognizes her own. She now finds herself drawn into the enactment and reflects Anna's body state. Almost as if mirror images of each other, they hang together, twisted by a seemingly unresolved tension. It is a timeless experience that moves through and beyond personal pain. They remain suspended together, moving only slightly, crying silently until both know that something has shifted. Although the issue is not resolved, there is a feeling of completion and relief. A struggle known by each of them individually, and by many women, has been seen and touched. A synchronistic moment has occurred. When they are ready to talk, the sense of mutuality remains strong. Rather than interpreting, they each tell about their own experience of the movement.[99]

3. *Dearmoring.* Here the therapist intends to actively move against the patient's somatic defense system through pressure that can range from light touch to deep massage. Anita Greene describes this kind of touching, which is Reich's direct contribution to body therapy:

> My long experience with body work has demonstrated to me how certain images and memories, both positive and negative, are so imprisoned in body tissue that they may never appear in the analytical work until released through touch. On one occasion as I massaged a pocket of tension in a young woman's back, she burst into tears and remembered, at age 9, digging a grave for a beloved pet and swearing over its small body that she would never drink. The patient had been unaware until that moment of how intensely she had been affected by her father's alcoholism.[100]

Finally, gratification as a motive in touching is such a complex issue that it will be discussed in some detail.

Gratification in Analysis

One of the major theoretical issues for the integration of analysis and touch is the question of whether gratification is required in the healing process.

Common to all depth therapies is the expectation that the patient will reexperience feeling-toned complexes in some intensity before transformation can take place. This was Freud's and Breuer's basic tenet, and it was fundamental to Jung's complex theory. The reliving of feeling experiences in the safety of the analytic *temenos* is believed to be related to the healing process, which takes place when the archetypal energies associated with the complex are awakened; through the connection with those energies reflected by the analyst, the patient begins to recognize and experience emotionally the activation of the archetypal energies of the Self which form the core of the complex.

Intellectual recognition of complexes without the emotional experience does not activate movement at the level of the archetypes, which are always plugged into instinctual, feeling processes. But when the complex is activated at the deep feeling levels, the energy of the Self, covering as it does the full spectrum from the instinctual to the spiritual, enriches the ego and expands the field of consciousness, thereby presenting new adaptations and solutions to wounding experiences through the transcendent function. (This is why analysis is lengthy, and why the transformation of complexes usually does not take place in quicker, more directive types of psychotherapy.) The ego is then more able to move from the pain and to find new attitudes toward old problems and impasses. These solutions may be predominantly on a spiritual level or on an instinctual level, or on both.

Gratifying Needs Symbolically

The theory of treatment described above implies that needs (as part of feeling-toned complexes) must be experienced by the patient, but does not imply that they must be gratified directly. The individuation process, while seeking consciousness and a need for balance, might lead one to live out one's life in a way that seems unbalanced to the outside observer or collective. In the Jungian view of individuation, perfection is not the goal but rather completion or wholeness. This means that one may come to see that some infantile needs and some current needs can never be satisfied at the instinctual level.

However, the tension of these ungratified desires can be experienced and withstood while the individuation process proceeds. It is in the blocking of awareness that the instinctual needs become distorted and start to sicken us—an attempt to compensate a too one-sided consciousness. In the case of sexuality from this point of view, the notion that heterosexual genital gratification must be lived out to achieve self-actualization does not hold, in contrast to theoretical approaches reducing wholeness to efficient distribution of psychic energy, such as in Reichian theory. If one can make conscious and contain one's capacity for sexuality, gratification is not necessary for self-actualization. However, if not recognized, sexual impulses become compensatory and compulsive to the degree of repression. While the individual may not experience his or her full awareness of sexual power in the world of outer relatedness, transformation of the personality is still possible,[101] but the body's needs must be recognized, not repressed.

Sacrifice which carries a meaning, such as celibacy, is a viable alternative to gratification. Crucial to this viewpoint is the acceptance of the symbolic process to evoke the healing properties of the archetype. Goodheart considers symbolizing to be a result of the patient being frustrated by the inability to re-obtain the "incestuous and natural aberrant union for which part of his or her unconscious life clamors," while receiving the understanding of the analyst who takes a "firm stance toward the awakening and emergence of *imaginatio.*"[102] He acknowledges Jung as first describing this enormous step toward freeing the ego from the unconscious.

Gratifying Needs Through Embodiment

On the other hand, some therapeutic models maintain that health cannot be achieved until early damage to the body and psyche (damage which continues to be apparent in the cells of the body and continues to need defending against by splitting from consciousness and muscular armoring) can be uncovered, relived and healed through gratification on a primitive level by touch.

Child analysts such as D.W. Winnicott contend that a child of any age who needs to be held affectionately is seeking a physical form of loving which was given naturally in the womb.[103] In this model it is not enough to be conscious of the early pain of deprivation, but it is necessary that early wounding be repaired. This may occur through reparenting physically and emotionally by touching and holding at a pregenital level, as one would touch and hold a small child, so that the muscular armoring gives way to the free flow of energy into the deprived tissues of the body. Until then, presumably the armoring against early pain must continue and the person will be thwarted in his or her capacity to relate to other beings at that level of awareness. Greene says:

> We have all experienced how insight into a complex and its archetypal images is often not sufficient to change the compulsive nature of an associated behavior that has its roots in the very structure of the body. Jung felt that "the durability of a complex is guaranteed by its continually active feeling-tone. If the feeling tone is extinguished, the complex is extinguished with it." Most body- and movement-oriented therapies are based on the assumption that the body has a long memory.[104]

Woodman describes the compensatory process as follows:

> The body is suspicious and terrified, and only gradually can it learn to trust its own instincts and discipline them into a firm steady base for the maturing psyche. Unless the body knows it is loved, that its responses are acceptable, the psyche does not have the ground of certainty in the instincts that it requires; sooner or later in the analysis the person will become stuck because the ego is afraid to trust; at the point of surrender the ego becomes paralyzed. Unless the body knows that there are inner loving arms strong enough to contain it, however fierce or broken it may be, it will hang onto its own rigidity in an effort to survive. That rigidity is echoed in the rigidity of the persona and the ego.[105]

Malcolm Brown says the process of creatively disintegrative regression is necessary to the healing process:

Some feel regression is not necessary, but, on the contrary, weakening. But the challenge to all psychotherapy is to transform the regulative system of the body away from the corticospinal circuit to a Self-regulated system.[106]

It may be that some patients cannot even become aware of the needs of their bodies because of defensive armoring against feeling needs in general. In this case, how do we enable the ego to assimilate the repressed energies until they can at least be recognized? There seems to be an argument here for the need for touch to open the defensive person to the *possibility* of recognizing, if not gratifying, bodily needs.

To some extent the ego of the patient may learn to trust and to open to greater awareness of the body's needs through the example of the containing attitude of the analyst, who receives the tension and insists on the symbolic transformation of pain; but there may be instances in which actual body contact is needed in order for the patient to trust, and for the messages from the body to come into awareness. This is a point of theoretical debate. Some analysts, like Greene and Woodman, argue for the support of some natural gratification of body needs as essential to healing. Others, such as Goodheart, consider that the therapist's acting out the needs of the patient on a physical level, rather than symbolically, represents an "aberrant union and clinging to the material corporeality of the mother."[107]

Individual Differences in the Need for Gratification

Damage in early infancy can be compensated for in healthy adults, so it is conceivable that many of us function well without any awareness of how wounded we were as infants. Yet the residue of early damage may play itself out in complexes which could be resolved if we could get to deeper experiences in analysis.

It may be that those who were most damaged in early infancy most require body work for healing to take place. Need plus motivation complicates the decision about who needs a gratification-oriented analysis. For example, some persons are satisfied to accept limitations of their functioning, while others are motivated to push through very strong resistance at the physiological level in order to become more conscious. In the example of Lee, who was not given any physical expressions of affection by her mother, we see how a woman could go through life apparently well integrated, productive and creative, and still be suffering from intense deprivation of her affectional needs. Her defenses against longing for affection keep her at a distance from her ability to gratify other needs, such as the need to express anger and sexuality.

As analysts we continue to push the limits of what is treatable. There was a time when I was taught that certain personality types were not amenable to analysis, but as the dynamics of certain disorders become more clearly conceptualized, more patients become accessible to the analytic method. I believe that as our sophistication about the language of the body increases, more patients will make dramatic changes in opening their physiological defenses. It may be that we need the symbolizing model of analysis for some patients, touching to facilitate awareness for others, and the gratification model for others.

It is interesting that Goodheart, who favors the exclusively symbolic mode, focuses on Jung's references to the negative mother, whereas Greene and Woodman, who favor the tactile mode, focus on the positive aspects of the Great Mother in their writing. This suggests to me that a preference for certain kinds of interventions exists in the personality of the therapist and colors his or her theoretical orientation, as Jung pointed out in explaining the differences between Freud, Adler and himself.[108]

Gratification of the Patient's Need for Contact, Containment, Parenting, Affection and Sex

Returning to our categorization of kinds of touch we find the following motives for gratifying patients:

Providing contact. A good bit of unconscious touching by therapists is probably motivated by this consideration, for instance handshaking and the backpat. Whitmont describes this as a "channel of relatedness for contact-starved adults."[109] Greene quotes London analyst Camilla Bosanquet, who suggests that if analysts do not touch, they may deprive patients of a valuable means of communication, including associations to touching and being touched. Greene adds:

> In my experience touch provides many patients with more direct access to the damaged roots of their undeveloped feeling potential, and at the same time, opens a pathway to the restoration of their paralyzed or dissociated potential.[110]

Providing affection. This takes "providing contact" a step farther into emotional gratification, including expressing affection toward the patient by hugging, kissing, stroking and similar expressions of tenderness which are not sexually motivated.

Providing containment. The analyst may physically hold a patient who is reliving terror or grief from early trauma, in order to give the patient enough support to stay in the pain of the experience; otherwise, some relived pain creates so much anxiety that it can never be fully reexperienced but quickly falls back into the shadow.

Providing parenting. Woodman describes this:

> Analysis attempts to uncover the complexes in which repressed energy is locked. If the analysand has a relatively harmonious body/psyche relationship, the shadow material is obvious in the dreams. In many people, however, body and psyche were split apart at a very early age. . . .
>
>   Body work, which must be handled with considerable patience and love, reaches out to that lost infant whose little body—violent, tender, sure—was never allowed to develop.[111]

Gratification of sexual needs. It is generally accepted in analytical psychology that whatever the analyst's position regarding pregenital gratification may be, she or he will not follow through with gratification at the genital level. Many studies indicate the undesirability of gratifying patients' sexual needs. Schwartz-Salant has cited some of them in his essay "Archetypal Factors Underlying Sexual Acting-Out in the Transference/Countertransference Process," which takes this subject out of the realm of morality to examine it symbolically.[112] (This is discussed further in the next section, Touch and Transference.)

Gratification of the Analyst's Needs

In my opinion, touch that is motivated by the analyst's need for gratification is *never* justified, and when it is done amounts to exploitation of the patient. Every analyst, but especially one who engages in body therapy, must be able to experience and contain his or her own pregenital and genital impulses, both homosexual and heterosexual. This point is stressed by body therapists because of the physical pressure put on the transference-countertransference by physical proximity; however, because the possibility of sexual activity is such a conscious factor, the probability of the analyst's being seduced is arguably far less than in traditional analysis.

Among Jungian analysts the consensus is that sexual acting out in analysis is damaging to the soul of both patient and analyst. Yet, as Schwartz-Salant points out, a need for "kinship libido" (Jung's term) is a special energy which may be compulsively and unconsciously sought through sexuality. This energy arises from the conjoining experiences in a deeply moving transference-countertransference process, and cannot be reduced to infantile personal complexes of the analyst and patient. To repress this energy without trying to understand it would mean foregoing its transformation. Schwartz-Salant concludes:

> We need to educate ourselves to the imaginal nature of the *coniunctio* so that we will be in a position to integrate this shadow of our profession. Only then will we have a chance for transformation rather than repression, and only then will we respect the mystery of both sexuality and spirit, body and soul.[113]

While working with the body one is usually confronted at some point with the sexual aspects of the patient. Awareness of sexuality becomes a very natural part of the process of becoming conscious of the body; the therapist who is managing his or her own sexual energy well can observe the emergence of sexuality in the patient without getting compulsively caught up in his or her own sexual complexes, just as a healthy parent can encourge a child's sexual development without participation. It is when the sexual desires of the analyst are ignored and repressed that compulsive acting out is most likely to occur.

When sexual needs of the patient are the focus of therapy, the therapist can be accepting and supportive of the patient's sexual energy, can feel complimented by the patient's seductive attention, but at the same time can be firm and clear about telling the patient that those energies will not be acted out between them. It amounts to the analyst saying "no" to the patient and to herself or himself, just as one would in any inappropriate social milieu. This leaves analyst and patient free to explore in fantasy what a sexual encounter between them would mean, and also to appreciate the *coniunctio* experience in the subtle body, or somatic unconscious, as described by Schwartz-Salant.[114]

Touch and Transference

In his essay, "The Psychology of the Transference," Jung described the complexity of the psychological interaction between the two partners in an analysis—the transference-countertransference relationship.[115] Besides what happens between the two on a conscious level, unconscious factors are also active, though unexpressed. Jung was among the first to insist on the importance of a training analysis for every analyst, and now it is required in every school of depth psychology that the candidates undergo a personal analysis of some years' duration. This is to decrease the possibility that the analyst will influence the analysis unconsciously due to being unaware of his or her own complexes.

It is the strong bond that develops between analyst and analysand that makes it possible for complexes to be experienced at a deep instinctual level and not just intellectually. But this healing bond or "kinship libido" creates risks for both.

One of the arguments raised against the use of touch in analysis is that touching the patient will so complicate and overstimulate the transference that analysis will become impossible. I do not believe this to be true and as far as I have been able to tell, facts do not bear this out.

Speaking for nonverbal techniques in general, Whitmont writes:

> Contrary to the usual expectation, the inclusion of non-verbal enactment does not complicate transference problems, but tends to help

in working them out. It does so by clarifying, through direct experience, the qualities of transference and countertransference. Mutual resistances and their unconscious motives are brought into focus.[116]

Transference-countertransference problems in body therapy may reflect a lack of experience on the part of the therapist. It is possible to be too "at ease" with body work, approaching it with enthusiasm and lack of restraint or caution about its effect on the other because it looks relatively easy.

In this era of physical fitness enthusiasm, we are encouraged to plunge into exercise and massage with little understanding of the long-term physiological ramifications. We are likewise led to believe, by collective standards, that it is permissible to intrude physically and sexually on others with no long-range consequences. Because of the power of the transference, the analyst's ethical responsibility to consider with care and forethought the meaning of body work to the patient has been rightly stressed.

In touching the patient we very easily open up the possibility of preverbal transferences. That is, by physical contact when the patient is in a regressed, nondefended state, we set up conditions whereby the patient may fuse with the analyst as an infant would, at such an early level that it cannot be conceptualized in words. Intense dependency needs are often evoked which are not entirely in the patient's awareness, and are not spoken of unless the therapist can bring them forth. Sometimes these early needs can appear to the patient as strong sexual attraction to the therapist. Skill and experience on the part of the therapist is needed to discern the patient's true needs.

The misuse of power, especially with regard to sexual acting out, reveals the shadow of analysis. Schwartz-Salant has described the archetypal elements in the attraction toward sexual acting out in therapy as "a signal that the energies necessary for the *coniunctio* have not yet been sufficiently constellated and certainly not integrated".

> The fact that the *coniunctio* can happen in the here and now, with healing results, accounts for the motive behind a good deal of sexual acting-out. This behavior can be seen as a kind of forced sexual magic stemming from split-off parts of the analyst's and analysand's psyche, which are mingled with archetypal factors.[117]

Whitmont explains that sexual transference may really be a masked need to have one's reality affirmed by the therapist in a concrete experience. To dismiss this need or treat it as purely sexual is to possibly increase resistance, depression and sexualization, which then may "play havoc with transference and countertransference."[118]

In a relationship where passing the box of Kleenex can be ill-advised at certain times, touching the patient's body undoubtedly can create a complex web of repercussions. This is no reason to eschew touching. It means, however, that the therapist's goals and reasons must be absolutely clear and uncomplicated by his or her own personal needs.

Mario Jacoby, in *The Analytic Encounter: Transference and Human Relationship,* describes the paradoxical nature of analysis— its aim being to live one's nature, although becoming conscious often seems to work against nature.[119] In this paradoxical milieu the analyst's function is to serve the process of individuation, not one's own ego choices for the patient. In the struggle with difficult transference problems, Jung felt that the analyst worked not only for the patient's welfare, but for the good of his or her own soul, "and in so doing he is perhaps laying an infinitesimal grain in the scales of humanity's soul. Small and invisible as this contribution may be, it is yet an *opus magnum.*"[120]

In the case of Lee, there were many times when I touched and massaged her body without any indication from her, or from my own imagery and feelings, of a sexual connection. Then there were times when sexual fantasies would come into my awareness, which I would notice without commenting on. I could imagine at a later stage revealing my fantasies to her at the time of their occurrence, but that was not appropriate now.

On one occasion I noted in my written summary after the session that my sexual feelings came through strongly. Lee, of course, never saw these notes. Ten days later Lee admitted sheepishly that she had avoided telling me a dream recently, but thought she had better stop suppressing it. She read it to me:

> In the dream, I was lying prone on Del's sofa bed, and she was stroking or massaging my upper thighs and lower back. She began

touching my vagina, and then inserted her fingers and continued the stroking. It was pleasurable to me, but I felt a deep resistance to this, with the sense that it was not appropriate for the analytic session. When I woke I still felt I couldn't record the dream or report it for a long time after having it.

This led to a discussion about the suppression of her sexual feelings in general and with her husband, and a more detailed account of her past experience. Lee spent a good bit of time in that session talking about her feelings for me, whom she saw as "a good friend, sometimes mothering, sometimes a priestess or sorceress who has access to the unconscious in a way that I don't know about yet." During this session she realized how lonely her life had been and how seldom she had ever felt taken care of. Always she did the caretaking. She was able to feel this strongly and cried deeply.

From this incident one can see clearly the communication of sexuality without a word being said or any overt sexual touching. I believe this process takes place in every healthy parent-child relationship. As I see it, the mother automatically transmits her accepting attitude (or the reverse) toward the erogenous zones of her child. She physically permeates her child with her own sexuality, which in the healthy adult woman is a feminine, Yin energy—containing, languorous, permissive, sensuous. The father, also without overt sexual touching, transmits (usually) his masculine Yang energy, which is experienced by the child as assertive, penetrating, vigorously stimulating.

The healthy child has been accepted and contained at all developmental levels and in all erogenous zones. Therapists repeat or correct this process, often at a level outside of their awareness. When I was applying gentle pressure on Lee's lower abdomen I was generating in her a permissiveness to feel the energy in her entire pelvis, which manifested itself in a dream of my penetrating her vagina. This can be experienced also through a tone of voice, an expression in the eyes, by one who is receptive. To an armored person, more deliberate cues are necessary.

One of the problems Lee had had since having a hysterectomy ten years before was that during intercourse she always experienced pain. This contributed more negativity to her already less-than-enthusiastic reaction to sex. Soon after the above sexual dream, Lee came in with the remarkable news that intercourse with her husband was no longer painful. After that she found it easier to relax and to enjoy being touched. The pain did not return.

Jung insisted that the unconscious be perceived as containing not only repressed contents, but also undeveloped potentialities. I believe that some of this potential can never be brought to light without body therapy.

Lee could not have begun her inner work with body therapy. She had to begin with her very strongly introverted intuitive mind, and even after several months of body work her dreams revealed some resistance, especially from masculine figures. Consciously this took the form of a fixed belief that, since she and her husband had made a good adjustment to her lack of libido and to her obesity, any changes might "rock the boat" too drastically. My invasion of her privacy through touch she came slowly to accept and trust, but it took years to build that trust, which brings us to the next issue, one of timing and the need for processing over an adequate period of time.

Touch and Timing in Analysis

Some complexes are especially resistant to resolution, such as those involving pain incurred at a very early age, those involving traumas of which one is unaware, complexes based on a long-term life style which is unbalanced, etc. How such complexes can be resolved, how quickly and how deeply, raises many complex questions.

For example, one question involves the amount of time needed to insure a substantial change in a complex at a meaningful level of psychic awareness. Some critics of analysis point to the apparent possibility that a flash of insight during a "peak experience" or marathon workshop can accomplish what would take years in analysis. Analysts might question whether such an experience involves the resolution of a complex—its integration and assimilation—or simply the exchange of one complex for another.

One example of the kinds of theory being generated around this issue is articulated by Joseph Masterson. In *Countertransference and Psychotherapeutic Techniques* he states that the borderline and narcissistic disorders cannot achieve authentic affective changes as long as there is not consistent confrontation of the patient's defense maneuvers before interpretation occurs. Any acting out of the "rewarding object-relations unit" by the therapist before the abandonment depression is resolved contributes to resistance and prevents real change.[121] Wilhelm Reich said this half a century ago in his book *Character Analysis*—the neurotic resistances must be treated first. In contrast, Arthur Janov claims to eliminate these defenses through psychic and physical deprivation in a few weeks. While most body therapists do not make such exaggerated claims, there is still the implication that something can occur through attention to the somatic defenses that cannot occur through verbalization. To my knowledge we have no firm data to compare the value of various methods of "working through" pain in terms of the amount of time needed to heal early wounds.

Many analysts believe, with Masterson, that manipulative techniques involving assertive input from the therapist result in intellectualization that masks some entrenched resistance which becomes apparent when the rewarding-object is withdrawn. Yet Chodorow points out that Jung used "impressive" as well as "expressive" techniques, and there can be times where "a behavioral approach to psychic change . . . has a place in the individuation process."[122] Whitmont proposes that a new form of ego, "directly self- and inner-determined and motivated," is emerging in our time to replace the rational, patriarchal ego, predominantly outer-directed. This newly evolving ego is closer to affect and emotion than to the rational frame of reference. "If analysis is to reach out into this deepening of experience," he writes, "it cannot continue to limit itself to verbal and interpretive methods."[123]

While all agree that authentic affect must occur at the deepest level of the psyche, there is no clear agreement on the means of evoking that level of emotion, nor on the length of time needed to insure the integration of strong affect.

What *is* authentic change at the physiological level? We know that psychotherapy, but also biofeedback, can affect significant changes in the body's functioning, as reflected in changes in blood pressure, digestion, respiration, etc. A strong affective state such as rage can be handled by providing the body with an opportunity to experience catharsis, as in bioenergetics. It can also be handled by assuming a meditative state, as well as by intellectual detachment and objectification. In all instances the physiological effects of rage disappear. Yet we don't know how these different methods of handling rage affect one on a long-term basis. The core of the affective personality seems to be reached through awareness on a level that can be influenced by deep breathing and deep relaxation. However, we do not know much about how that core is reached, nor do we know how it is affected when emotions are discharged through muscular actions which may affect changes in deep body tissues. It would appear on the surface that an attempt to alter consciousness by meditation is a form of escape from the body, yet a bodily change takes place.

In his "Commentary on *The Secret of the Golden Flower*," Jung points out that the way of the Yogi carries centuries of Eastern experience that Westerners cannot duplicate.[124] He saw the danger of taking a powerful force out of the context which nourished it, displacing it and planting it into an ego-oriented world where it could be abused and engaged in misdirected aims. This has certainly been done with yoga, with many resultant misconceptions.

To one point of view, Hatha Yoga is a spiritual ascent. As such it is limited in therapeutic usefulness and dangerous to those schizoid personalities or young people who need to establish a strong ego in the outer world. In a different context, but still appropriate here, Schwartz-Salant states that the introjection of the spirit archetype can promote the ego-Self relationship, but it is not necessarily an embodied ego-Self relationship; also it deflects attention away from shadow issues.[125]

From another point of view, Hatha Yoga is a descent into the very foundations of the sensation and feeling functions, the perfect antidote to our Western, overly cerebral, heroic attitudes. In fact Jung describes using yoga to ground himself in his turbulent period around 1913.[126]

Through regular practice of the yoga positions—the asanas—one can become aware of very specific body areas, which can then be contacted, slowly stretched and caused to relax over a period of time. This kind of work is best done with a trained teacher or guru.

While yoga does not come under my definition of body therapy because it does not include psychic reworking, the physical exercises may be helpful in the healing of early damage to the psyche in infancy and young childhood. Marcel Gaumond does not deny this, but questions the therapeutic value of yoga as a spiritual discipline:

> In spite of all its exercises designed to master physiological functions, yoga is a movement essentially motivated and sustained by spirituality. The yogi strives to accomplish a state of consciousness freed from the psycho-physiological structure and its temporal conditioning in order to attain union with Atman or Purusha (spirit, self, soul) through *Nirvana* (deliverance).

He contracts this with the goals of Eutony:

> [Gerda] Alexander, on the other hand, associates neither spiritual precept nor any form of doctrine with Eutony. For her, it is more a question of laying aside all speculations, prejudices and presuppositions concerning the body in order to be immediately and continually open to the physical experience, and all that surrounds and conditions it. The eutonist does not strive to master his body as he would an obstacle or instrument that would then become his means of reaching a higher spiritual reality. He rather strives to reach the body itself, in all its complexity, with the full weight of its reality. This he does so as to live in conscious harmony with his physical self.
>
> In spite of the absence of any spiritual concept that would sustain such unconditional attention to the body throughout its sufferings, implacable needs and unsuspected riches, there emanates from the conscious body a paradoxical mana, a self-expressive spiritual force which moves and acts at a profound level.[127]

We can arrive at spiritual awareness in different ways, including through a total acceptance of the body, and we can alter body consciousness to different degrees in the process of becoming spiritually oriented.

For example, let us assume that a patient is dealing with chronic rage. In the therapeutic process of "working through the complex," the following steps (not necessarily in this order) are necessary for consciousness to change on a characterological level:

1. Identification of the source of the affect. Example: the patient may identify one source of the rage to be the feeling of abandonment by mother.

2. Awareness of the resistance to feeling the affect that has been acquired over the course of a lifetime. Example: The patient becomes aware of how he or she has avoided recognizing that rage by fusing with mother.

3. Ability to give up the defensive behavior involved in this resistance. This is difficult to check, except as manifested in the transference. Example: Patient begins to risk differentiating from mother-dominated behavior, or begins to risk differentiating from the analyst, giving up the fusion which protects against rage.

4. Catharsis, implying full experience of the affect in the analytic session in relationship to the therapist. Example: Patient may express feelings of rage toward the analyst or toward mother in the presence of the analyst.

5. Desensitization to the affective responses required by sustained awareness of the affect. Even a lifetime of chronic rage will diminish by continued experience of it consciously.

Opinions differ on both what constitutes catharsis and how it manifests. One therapist may consider teariness a sufficient indication of full-blown affect, while to another nothing short of whole-body discharge of rage through pounding and screaming is genuinely cathartic. Do images of murderousness, untranslated into bodily manifestations such as adrenalin output and rapid breathing, amount to catharsis? Most body therapists would probably think not. And yet we know that image can heal.

The work by Carl and Stephanie Simonton on imagery in cancer patients suggests that visualizing what is happening at the site of cancerous growths in the body may be related to changing and even halting the cancer process.[128]

Behavior therapists and directive therapists such as Milton Erickson, who focus on behavioral change, argue that the other four steps, including awareness, are unnecessary and irrelevant for therapeutic change to occur. In other words, they argue that

behavioral change may or may not bring about alteration in awareness, as well as vice versa. They do not consider early memory to
be relevant to current levels of consciousness. Erickson and others
have shown that changes in behavior can be brought about by conscious manipulation of the patient's unconscious, outside the
patient's awareness.[129]

Reich's concept of trapped energy which must be controlled and
released for integration to occur, appears to be contradicted by the
concept of transcending tension through mental training and relaxation techniques. Psychological evidence of reduction in signs of
stress suggests that tension can be mediated through these
techniques without direct muscle contact. This in turn suggests that
with the correct mental attitude we can undo chronic areas of tension. But possibly these techniques are useful only for limited
change in acute tension. The techniques of yoga seem to by-pass
the very essence of Reich's area of concern. With these polar
attitudes toward the body, one wonders whether there is a need for
combination, or whether both are independently sufficient in themselves for healthy development.

Can we prepare ourselves to deal realistically with violence in
man and nature by relaxation? Perhaps the likelihood of aggressive
interaction is escalated by focusing on its actual release from the
muscles and tissues in energetic movement. Through meditation
and biofeedback we can teach people to raise body temperature, to
constrict or increase the flow of blood. Conceivably this could enable one, over time, to release a contracted muscle group which has
been overly tense for a prolonged period, even years. But whether
meditation is a better or simply another way to accomplish what is
aimed for in bioenergetics is not certain. I have posed this question
to body therapists and most feel that both attitudes are not only
viable but necessary. Malcolm Brown, for example, insists that the
peripheral muscular action has no long-term effects on the healing
process unless the vegetative energetic flow is established in the
vital organ centers, and some connection with the spirit enlivens
the body work.[130]

This is consistent with Jung's view of the identity of body and
psyche. Somehow the wedding of Western and Eastern approaches

to the body must occur. One way of accomplishing this is to combine body therapy techniques which elicit strong affect with interpretive analytic work to integrate the body work in the context of personal history. In addition relaxation and meditation techniques can be included as alternative ways of handling tension and as ways of contacting the unconscious complex and promoting its analytic resolution.

In the following section, part of the slow process of resolving certain very deep aspects of the mother complex through dream interpretation and body therapy is described.

Body Therapy and Dream Interpretation

My analysand Lee had many times during analysis verbalized disappointment, anger and hurt about her mother's abusive treatment of her as a child. Never were these memories accompanied by observable affect, for example tears or changes in color or breathing. In the third week of body therapy she brought a dream that involved a shadow figure, a passive, mother-dominated woman.

We talked about where she experienced that aspect of herself in life, and how it rarely emerged. I asked if it existed in our relationship. She admitted that she approached the body therapy like a "blinded" person, relying on me to see where we are going. She felt that she was able to yield to me in this way because I had already proven to her that I respected her deep-seated modesty, and was nurturing rather than confronting in my touch. She described how her mother absented herself emotionally and how she, Lee, would get sick or, when older, irritate mother to get a response from her. I asked her to allow herself to experience the pain she felt at her mother's inaccessibility, and she began to cry. As I applied mild pressure to her abdomen, chest and head, she sobbed vigorously, a great deal of energy being activated in the abdominal area.

A dream followed that session. Next time she came we did no body work, but analyzed the dream:

> My husband and I were traveling in the Northeast, in Connecticut and Massachusetts, and getting ready to take a ferry to Long Island.

We stopped for an overnight stay after passing through a worked-out rock quarry. On the map it was marked as "Rock Pit." I found out somehow after we'd stopped that there was a religious foundation in the rock quarry, or rather just beside it, with the buildings of the abbey worked around the rock of the pit. It was called "Beaulieu Abbey." It was said to be run by brothers called "hospitallers." I wanted to see it, but my husband said we couldn't and that we had to move on. I asked what we were moving on for. He said he wanted to get to the next place in plenty of time to scout out the tennis courts and general setup.

I didn't want to move on until I had seen this abbey. His reasons for wanting to leave seemed inconsequential to me and I thought I might never get back again to see this place. I was kind of digging in my heels as the dream ended.

The dream began as many of Lee's dreams did, with her and her husband traveling together. The Northeast represented to her a place of introversion and deep values. Rocks had also come up in Lee's imagination very frequently, and were associated with healing. Often she envisioned rocks in river beds and creeks as healing symbols, but in this dream the quarry was a dried-out area where the water of life did not flow.

With encouragement, she described the dream in more detail: "On the left I saw overhanging rock and on the right a space from which the rocks had been removed and a cavern led into the vault in different shades of grey stone. In the hole was blackness, and even from the car I felt afraid of falling in." Her awe in experiencing this cavern brought associations of fearful images: getting trapped in holes and psychic spaces from which one could not return, loss of control, the effects of drugs, etc. She recognized a degree of "not being in touch with the elemental." Yet this place, she said, held promise as a place of religious succor, a spiritual sanctuary. The brothers represented to her the possibility of remaining silent, focused, contemplative, and setting aside distractions of secular life. In contrast, her husband represented the part of her that was extroverted, often hurried and harried, oriented toward task-completion and duty. She said that the dream reminded her of "the sea journey . . . an image of transformation ahead," and brought clearly into reflection the shift in her relationship to her husband, her sureness about wanting to differentiate her way of doing their journey.

To me the dream illustrated her developing capacity to separate herself (feminine ego) from the extraverted animus (masculine principle), as well as from the devouring mother, so that she could see her feminine orientation much more clearly. It also illustrated her need to nurture and be nurtured in a deeply quiet and steady, unhurried way. She could now see the possibility of "standing on her own feet," and "holding ground" against those psychic forces which would lead her away from her essential, natural mode of being.

In the next analytic session we began with breathing exercises. I asked what her body wanted to do. "It wants to lie down." For ten minutes Lee was still and I kept my hands on her abdomen with a slight pressure during her exhalation, and letting-up during inhalation. Suddenly she remembered a dream: "I was trying to wrap up a baby. I couldn't get the blanket on."

There was a fifteen-minute silence, then, "I realized an architect had designed the room I was in. It was of perfect proportions and very comfortable."

I knew then that she was beginning to trust the body work for she had had many dreams of poorly supported structures in the past, and now she was in a safe room.

She thought about the previous dream of the black hole in the rock quarry and said, "I'm feeling energy in my feet—I feel secure enough to walk to the edge of the hole and look in. I'm not afraid of falling in. In the dream I was too afraid to step out of the car, but now I can imagine walking around it," which she did.

It seemed to me that the sobbing about mother's inaccessibility, the physical experience of such old longing, had brought about two consequences: 1) she was able to experience the black hole which was connected with a powerful place of healing, and 2) she was able to feel more grounded and secure in approaching that black hole. Here, it seems the principal release was related to a way of experiencing her loss of mother, which was far deeper and richer than anything she had previously allowed herself to know.

The theme of the hole in the earth returned several weeks later in a dream which took the image into a more differentiated and embodied form to become a grave:

> I was on the road that skirts the base of a mountain. I was with two young Indian girls. I was young too. We were all in our late teens or early twenties. We were traveling on this circular road around the mountain's base and stopping at various places. The Indian girls were very beautiful, both quiet and gentle, but not dull. There was a subtle humor about them and a fine sense of who they were, of being fully within themselves.
>
> We came to one place where there was a pretty paved brick area, like a sidewalk, or a place to wait beside the road, under some trees. Then we went on and came to a church and a burial ground where their people were buried. There was a larger brick pavement here, alongside the road. Above this, up the hillside, were the graves, and at the top was the brick church. All the churchyard was very green and damp, as though there was always a lot of rain. In some ways this setting made me think, later on, of the maraes in Tahiti—sacred places on the side of a mountain.
>
> Then we went into the church, and there were more graves inside. One of them was very unusual. It was set within a brick enclosure, almost like a bed. It was the grave of an old Indian woman. There was a surround of bricks on all four sides and a higher part at the head. The grave was covered with a slab of something brittle, like a piece of slate. It was cracked down the center. But one of the Indian girls pressed down on it with her hand, to show that it would yield a certain amount and no further, as though something supported it underneath so it wouldn't fall. She said it was a tradition among the Indians that if you lay down on this grave you would learn something very important about yourself. I didn't want to trust myself to it, fearing the brittle top would break and drop me down inside.
>
> There was a jukebox in the place, and one of the girls started it playing, as an accompaniment to their lying on the grave. The music it played was extraordinary, and I found myself dancing. I had no blouse on, and only a loose skirt that came just above my knees—a rather primitive Indian-like costume. I was dancing in a possessed, frenzied way, feeling a great flow of energy in my lower body, like highly charged sexual energy.
>
> And then some men walked in the door at the back of the church

and said something critical that stopped what we were doing and made me feel I should cover myself up. The man doing the talking said we shouldn't be behaving this way, that we should be more respectful of the place and behave decently. He was a very distasteful person—overbearing, physically unattractive, out of touch with any possible energies within himself that would cause him to dance in abandoned exuberance. I felt that his behavior would always be rooted in a sort of joyless nastiness.

I stopped dancing and put on a dressing gown, but I hated this man and felt myself to be bonded emotionally and spiritually to the Indian girls, knowing that we had not been disrespectful of the place but rather had been attempting to get in touch with the deepest traditional sources of energy in a way that came quite naturally and unbidden. I was mentally rebelling against everything the man was telling us, even though I couldn't act it out.

In this sequence the progressive movement of psychic image and body loosening appears clearly and poignantly related. The continual need to acknowledge resistance to change is also brought to consciousness in the form of the negative animus.

In addition to working on this dream verbally, I brought some Indian music to a session and we danced in the manner of her dream. There is much grounding movement in Indian dance; one stomps the feet and contacts Mother Earth quite vigorously, rhythmically, in a reciprocity of energy exchange between the body and the ground. We can see by the dream images that, while some resistance exists to "lying on the grave" in the prescribed ritual, some parts of Lee's psyche were already there. The movement to accept the ritualized surrender that will make a true communion with the earth possible is present and close to consciousness.

The image of the Indian girl pressing down on the grave with her hand duplicated one of the things I often did to her body in therapy. Again there is the invitation to approach the hole, which now has something covering it, but her fear of dropping down inside is still with her. That is, she is still not secure enough in her own identity to know that she could enter into the dark psychic spaces and come out again. But part of her, represented by the Indian girls, is grounded enough, wise enough, and secure enough to be able to do so.

In the body work we continued to concentrate on the energy center in the pelvis. In a typical session we had begun with some positions and movements to energize the pelvis and upper legs, squatting on the haunches and jumping up. Next, lying on the mattress, Lee stretched her whole body and I assisted by holding and stretching her arms above her head and then stretching her legs. Then, as I held her shoulders on the mattress, she kicked her legs vigorously. When she was exhausted, she lay quietly and said she imagined that she was lying on the Indian grave of her dream. I suggested that she see if she felt energy from the grave, and she allowed herself to feel a flow of energy between herself and the grave.

Then a new thing happened. For the first time in her years of therapy she made a request: "Put your hands under me." I supported her back with my hands under her. This she accepted wordlessly but with apparent relief. I felt it to be a significant breakthrough against strong inhibitions about asking for and accepting help.

The experience of having the back supported is extremely numinous to some people, particulary those who are staunchly independent and self-sufficient and keep a lot of tension in the back as a result of this attitude.

The psychic aspect of this work was reflected in two subsequent dreams, one in which she gave birth and one in which her mother had died and she was responsible for burying her.

What does the black hole in the earth represent to this woman? From her associations I believe it represents all kinds of fears, inadequacies, dark moods, confused states, altered states which are threatening to ego-control. For example, her tendency to become depressed to the point of not wanting to get out of bed; or her feeling that sexual relating would be uncomfortable and unfulfilling, or that she would be abandoned; or that her bodily processes would be found revolting and a cause for rejection. For several sessions we talked mainly about blood, feces, laziness, greed, and all manner of excess and incontinent behavior.

It is vitally important that we comprehend the profound meaning of contacting the dark energy represented (in Lee) by the black hole, if we as a species are to increase our capacity for relatedness—

relatedness with each other, with the animals, with God. It seems to be generally true that women have a greater willingness to deal with the dark forces nondefensively, not through any great virtue or lack of virtue, but because biology and social structures have forced women to be still—to see things through and process information in ways that men tend not to because they can more easily divert themselves.

It is more often women who confront negative issues, especially in relationships, who seek out psychotherapy, marital therapy, family therapy and medical help in general. It is enlightened women who begin to wonder, "Must the dragon always be slain? How can the dragon-energy be transformed?"

The dark energy represented by the black hole can be experienced more readily through relationship (where it is not easily avoided), but it also is experienced more positively *in* relationship. Bodily processes, such as Lee and I discussed in detail, have come to be considered disgusting and are shunned and hidden. As long as we refrain from lifting the veil from these presumed horrors and strive to remain pure, perfumed and sanitized, we barely tolerate each other's humanity.

In true intimacy the body, with its sounds, smells, pressures, functions, moisture, is accepted as our rightful place of being. In true relatedness the effects of age are not merely tolerated but cherished, for they mirror the sustaining nature of caring and enduring. In true relatedness illness is not just a nuisance but a source of compassion and comfort, as hospice workers well know.

As a girl I wondered if I could ever stand to be a mother. Of all the travails motherhood involves, the two I most dreaded were being awakened during the night and dealing with vomit. I didn't know about the nature of bonding—how concern for a child's distress (as well as an adult's) and love for that child's body can override one's personal discomfort.

This principle is also true of the psychic process in relationship. Anger, jealousy, envy and fear are basic emotions which have a place in intimacy. Often referred to as "negative emotions," implying that they are wrong or inferior, they are actually valuable and survival oriented. They guard the capacity for intimacy and warn us of dangers to relatedness. They are "hot" emotions, strongly physical, and their opposites have nothing to do with love, but with cool indifference. Rather than being repressed, they call out to be cultivated and refined.

We have come a long way in accepting sexuality, but are still in the Stone Age in relation to anger, jealousy, envy and fear. Without acknowledging the earthy feminine and the earthy masculine, our relationships remain superficial, based on collective niceties. Problems are not confronted and hammered out, but avoided, somatized, or ruled out, dictated against. "Don't cry!" "Don't talk back!" "No, you can't go to the bathroom!" These injunctions to children show up later in lack of relatedness to one's body and to others, in attitudes if not words. "I don't want to discuss it." "Leave me alone." "I'll never reach out again." "Shut up!"

Without openness of expression life and loving are constricted and constrained, and passion dies. Passion does not go out of marriage as a result of time or familiarity, but as a result of suppression. If at the first impasse or waning of affection we begin thinking of a way out or a new partner, we never enter the great mysteries. And without the capacity for compassion, negotiation in any area of human relations is thwarted.

The essential change in this segment of Lee's work was exposing and diminishing the power of the mother complex. Through the security established by the transference and the contact with archetypal images of the feminine in dreams, Lee was able to break out of old attitudes which had kept her bound with mother. The work on the negative inner man was also crucial, but will not be described here.

Touching and Analytic Training

The current training of Jungian analysts appears to reflect a change in attitudes toward the body in recent years. In fact, analysts from many theoretical schools who once questioned whether they should shake a patient's hand are now being taught to analyze and physically confront posture in weekend workshops such as those given by Arnold Mindell. At the 1984 conference of Jungian analysts in

New York, one whole day was devoted to body movement led by Marion Woodman, Joan Chodorow and Anita Greene. The Ghost Ranch Conference of Jungian analysts in 1985 had "The Body" as its theme.

Gerda Alexander does not allow beginning students to touch one another in Eutony training programs because the resulting emotionality distorts the development of sensory awareness. However, Arnold Mindell teaches a gentle way of confronting, verbally and physically, resistant areas of the body in order to intensify awareness in those parts. Freud's orthodox followers still maintain that deviation from the traditional verbal stance contaminates the analytic process with material from the analyst's psyche. Orgonomists and other body therapists like to point to the many patients who remain unchanged through years of classical four-times-a-week analysis.

Having myself been trained in psychoanalytic theory, then in the body therapies, and finally in analytical psychology, I can testify to the extremely inhibiting influence that analytic training, both Freudian and Jungian, can have on therapeutic style. From the constraints of a Freudian background I was in the habit of being extremely careful not to use suggestion, direction or exhortation in the slightest degree. But over many years of training workshops and individual sessions with Lowenian and Reichian therapists, during which I uncovered memories which had not emerged in analysis, I learned that their techniques were extremely effective and powerful paths to the somatic unconscious. I became much less restrained about using them with patients.

At first my own early Jungian training seemed to lend itself to the integration of analysis and body work. In the sixties and seventies some Jungian analysts perceived themselves as facilitators of the analysand's contacting the inner healing process, rather than focusing on the therapeutic relationship as the important healing factor. Analysands were encouraged to change analysts and experience different styles and genders of analysts, or to break up periods of analysis with periods of rest or abstinence from analytic work. The focus on intrapsychic relationships rather than on the transference made the incorporation of dance, movement and body work less complicated.

However, another trend in Jungian training today, paralleling interest in the body, is toward strengthening the *temenos* and intensifying the focus on transference-countertransference issues. With more emphasis on the transference now in analytic training, nonverbal techniques tend to be discouraged, and changing analysts or breaking up the period of analysis is not recommended. Goodheart writes:

> For some time, Jungians shared with other psychoanalytic approaches a fundamental assumption in their practices and in their case presentations of the myth of the innocent observer-interpreter. . . . Interpretations or comments to the patient take the form of pointing out patterns of behavior or "complex" or "unconscious" constellations that the patient is experiencing or struggling with. . . . They subtly presuppose the events within the patient as being at most tangentially linked to the therapist's behavior.[131]

He points out that we must now recognize that the patient's interaction is in response not only to the therapist's overt interventions, but also to the therapist's need for healing experiences. It remains to be seen how these two trends will be assimilated. As Anita Greene comments:

> Jungians actively encourage their patients to paint, sculpt, or write out their confrontations with the unconscious. In general, though, Jungians have little understanding of how sensory awareness and body experience can strengthen the ego, activate the personal layer of the unconscious, and enable many patients to contact archetypal levels of energy and image that have been previously blocked or negativized.[132]

This statement supports my observation that many analysts belong to a generation who received little touching or body contact with family members or friends while growing up. Under such circumstances touching of any kind may be associated, or even equated, with sexual stimulation. The predominance of patriarchal values has relegated feminine values (such as enjoyment of close physical proximity and nurturing touch) to the shadow. Because of this many analysts feel guilty or awkward about touching patients, even when their motivation is to dearmor or provide containment and not gratification. Patients also may interpret touching as seduction or invasion. Analysts who are not connected with their own somatic awareness tend to experience any kind of touching as a form of gratification rather than an exploratory, opening technique; they may also misjudge the effect of their touch on the patient.

Therefore the major prerequisite for training as a body therapist is to have had experience as a patient in body therapy, to overcome one's own blocks and armors to feeling, and to know one's own capabilities and limits. At this point in the development of body therapy there are no standards or guidelines for training, except in dance therapy programs. Analysts have to depend on their own judgment and experience, and approach body work with a healthy degree of humility, good judgment and ethical reponsibility.

Setting standards for the training of psychotherapists has always been a thorny problem.[133] Training as a body therapist is even less institutionalized than classical analytic training. There are academic dance therapy programs and institutes for bioenergetic and Reichian methods. Therapeutic skills can be taught to a certain extent. Except for some behavioristic techniques, however, there is an element of art to psychotherapy. No amount of formal classwork or supervision can guarantee the artistic skills needed by an analyst or body therapist.

No matter how much analytic training one has, it is hard to anticipate some of the resistances that arise in the use of body methods. This may be due to the fact that in some ways the energy required of an analyst is different and counterproductive to the energy required of a body therapist. This is my own experience and is corroborated by other therapists with whom I have discussed this issue. It is one thing to be aware of one's own physical sensations and to be aware of the interaction between patient and therapist in terms of somatic cues. It is quite another thing to shift frames of reference in a way that enables one to leave the verbal, interpretive mode and to mobilize the energy to actually move in a session.

This mode of being prepared to move and take action may constellate the shadow side of the analyst. Consciously preoccupied with the psyche in a receptive attitude, the analyst may anticipate and fear the enantiodromia of that conscious orientation. He or she may fear the eruption of its opposite in a desire for power or for a primitive sexual acting out. The more conscious one can be about what the body is saying at all times, the less likely one is to fall into this enantiodromian enactment of the shadow. Experienced body therapists know there is a very distinct line between touching a patient with intentions of gratification and touching a patient with intentions of therapeutic intervention. It is the therapist's familarity with his or her own feelings and sensations that makes this distinction possible. The body therapist's most significant tools are personal body awareness as well as intuition and a clear ethical stance.

In working with Lee I found myself calling on my experience with methods of direct touch rather than dance movement. I was not following any prescribed procedures or guidelines in approaching Lee's body. I was guided mostly by her dreams and my intuition. Because of her rich dream material and my empathy with her body I was able to shift between the seated, verbal, interpretive mode and the active, touching, nonverbal mode.

In contrast, Joan, another patient, was an artistic woman who enjoyed expressing herself through movement. I could sit back and witness Joan's active imagination through dance movement, as Chodorow describes in her paper given at the 1985 Ghost Ranch Conference.[134]

For example, once Joan was struggling with feelings of shame and embarrassment while trying to tell me about some strong humanitarian feelings that had been inundating her recently. We discussed possible sources of the embarrassment, without bringing about much change in the intensity of the discomfort. Noting the tension in her body, I asked Joan where she felt the greatest shame and discomfort. Joan said her chest felt more tight and protected. I asked her to demonstrate this discomfort in movement. She began to hunch over, contracting her chest in a more exaggerated way, and folding her arms over her chest. Gradually she began to open her arms to expose her chest. When she did so she immediately reeled back and contracted as if receiving a blow. This movement was repeated many times until she began to initiate very strong arm and pelvic movements; gradually she was able to expose her chest more and more without appearing to suffer. This was followed by a joyful kind of dance.

Later Joan described her experience as wanting to "open her heart," but each time she exposed her chest she would feel vulnerable to being beaten severely by her mother. She was able to summon energy from the pelvis and upper back to produce the arm and pelvic thrusts, to come to the defense of the chest and gradually open it without fear. Then she was able to feel a strong flow of energy from the chest, a sense of oneness with mankind without embarrassment, and a desire to move about in a free-spirited dance.

In subsequent sessions Joan's experience was verbally processed with associations about her relationship with her mother, accompanied by a noticeable transfer of power from mother to self.

Lee did not have the flexibility nor the inspiration for such expressiveness. Her body called out for touch to awaken and stimulate it. Her fire was hidden, but dreams told us it yearned for discovery; it smoked under the floorboards and seeped through the cracks. I listened for clues in her breathing, in her fantasies and dream images, and in the tension/release experience perceived through my hands, in deciding where and with what kind of pressure to touch her body. And then I watched her consequent behavior and dreams for affirmative or negative responses to what we had done.

Formalized professions do not always have the last or complete word on their subject matter. There are mysteries involving breath and its relationship to energy and anxiety that medical schools do not teach. Diets prescribed by psychic nutritionists seem to have as much validity for some individuals as those prescribed by conventional medical practitioners for treatment of certain disorders. Standards for psychotherapists are terribly difficult to establish. It is easy to be caught on the horns of ignorance and inflation by trying to prepare oneself as a body therapist.

Mindell describes how for years, before arriving at his approach to the body from a viewpoint that sees the dreambody as hovering "between body sensation and mythical visualization," he prepared himself for the work:

Before I felt at home in the world of dreams I had to suffer through thousands of hours of dream analysis, labor over methods of imagination, association, and amplification. Tuning into body phenomena also requires a great deal of expertise.[135]

As the situation now stands, each analyst must evaluate his or her own ability and readiness to use body techniques. As a group, analysts need to give more thought and research to how to handle the problems provoked by shifting between the verbal interpretive mode and the nonverbal active mode.

Body Therapy and Jungian Typology

Jung's model of psychological types includes two major orientations, introversion and extraversion. Jung believed that an individual is predisposed toward one of these attitudes from birth, although to some extent the orientation can be influenced by the environment. Generally, however, we remain oriented throughout life toward inner experiences (introversion) or toward experiences in the outer world (extraversion).

In Jung's schema, each of these orientations is associated with four functions or ways of processing information. The "rational" functions, thinking and feeling, have to do with making judgments about the data we receive. The "irrational" functions, intuition and sensation, have to do with how we perceive, how we take in the data.[136]

Jung thought that each person developed one of these four functions best and relied consciously on it as a way of processing information, while the other three functions remained less developed. If one of the rational functions was best developed or "dominant," the other rational function would be the least developed or most unconscious and "inferior." For example, if one tends to relate to the available information by thinking about it and judging its value according to whether it makes sense, whether it is logically consistent, right and true, one's thinking function is dominant, and one is unlikely to give much conscious energy to deciding how one feels about the data; therefore the feeling function will be undeveloped and largely an unconscious influence.

Similarly, if one tends to relate to data primarily by simply experiencing what is perceived through the five physical senses, giving conscious attention to noticing and appreciating details, then the irrational sensation function is dominant. In that case the other irrational function, intuition—concerned with intangible cues, hunches, trends and possibilities—will be relatively unconscious and inferior.

In each person one orienting attitude, extraversion or introversion, will predominate, as will one function, reflected in the conscious behavior. This enables us to describe a person as, for instance, an "extraverted intuitive," or "introverted feeling type," and so on through eight possible combinations. In addition, whatever one's main function, there is usually a helping function of the opposite nature which is also relatively conscious, called the auxiliary function. That is, if the dominant function is irrational intuition, one of the two rational functions, thinking or feeling, will generally be quite well developed; and if a rational function is dominant, the auxiliary function will be irrational. This results in sixteen major types, for example "introverted intuitive feeling," "extraverted sensation thinking," and so on.

Jung recognized that we had more to learn about the connection between typology and psychotherapeutic methods: "The difficult task of creating a psychology which will be equally joined to [the different types] must be reserved for the future."[137] In the present context, a central concern is whether there is a correlation between the typology of the therapist and the attraction to body therapy.

Since body work is very sensual it would seem likely that it would attract therapists whose sensation function is well developed, or alternatively intuitives for whom sensation, being inferior, is numinous. As for the rational or judgment functions, it seems equally possible to do body work from a framework of thinking or feeling. It is my observation that most dance therapists have a dominant feeling function, reflected in their use of music. Dance movement therapy does not generally attract thinking types, and perhaps for that reason has not been described very accurately until recently.

Anita Greene has underlined the connection between her typology and body work:

My deep need for body consciousness is undoubtedly related to my own typology. All the Jungian types need body awareness, but as an introverted sensate, I am especially confronted by the nonverbal character and slow nature of my own process. Emma Jung, also an introverted sensate, likened this type of person to a highly sensitized photographic plate that receives images indiscriminately and often intensely. Impressions tend to divorce themselves from the outer object and sink into the depths of the psyche. Unless there is some means of artistic expression, the impressions get lost and hold the person a prisoner under their fascinating spell.[138]

Marion Woodman also discusses typology:

Many intuitives who have trusted their intuitive powers all their lives realize through body work that their bodies are just as intuitive as their psyches. . . . Intense body response has to be taken into consideration in analysis because the feeling function is so crucial to ego development. If a person is doing his/her best to establish a standpoint based on authentic feeling, and trying to develop the courage to act on that standpoint, then the body must reenforce that stand.[139]

According to Arnold Mindell's classification of the sensing orientation into visual, aural, kinesthetic and proprioceptive, it is likely that the majority of body therapists, particularly dancers, are essentially kinesthetically oriented.

Some body therapists come to their specialty through the need to work on an infirmity (Gerda Alexander, Franz Alexander, Mindell); others, like Pesso and Brown, combined their artistic careers (dance and voice respectively) with intuitive and psychotherapeutic skills.

Mindell combined his background in physics along with an illness to develop his interest in the dreambody. In my own case I was driven by infertility to explore ways to overcome my body's block to pregnancy. Physical examinations revealed no apparent reason for my failure to become impregnated. After years of analytical work on the probable complexes involved in this condition I turned to body therapy as a way of altering the deepest aspects of the reproductive system. Finally I did become pregnant, although I cannot be sure that any one therapy can be credited with the breakthrough. It was a problem I worked on at every possible level, physical, psychological and spiritual. I then was moved to try to combine body therapy with my love for dance and music.

As for introversion-extraversion, each attitude has certain advantages to the body therapist. The introverted therapist will find it easier to inspire patients to communicate with their deepest experiences through somatic focusing. Nevertheless, there is an assertiveness required of the body therapist which is not required of the verbal therapist and is difficult for introverts to assume. An extraverted, intervening focus with a new ethical shift is required of the introvert. It can be learned, however.

For many analysts, moving out of their own chair is very difficult. One style is to sit on the floor with patients from the beginning. Then when movement seems warranted, it is no big effort or surprise. When I present floor-sitting as a way of working that helps to break up rigid habit patterns at the start, most accept it readily. Timing is crucial, and I no longer urge patients to do anything physical that they have the slightest resistance to doing. With Lee, I introduced the use of the mattress at the beginning of doing body work. Working on the unpadded floor does not allow for vigorous kicking and pounding. In my office I have a sofa that opens easily into a bed, allowing for full-bodied "temper tantrums." Lee was not ready for that type of expression when we began, but my intuition told me that she would be in the near future, and I lay the groundwork by getting her used to working on a mattress.

Lee was a thinking type, I a feeling type. To work physically with her I had to overcome some reticence in myself as well as in her. However, with Joan, also a feeling type and a dancer, I experienced no reticence in encouraging her body movement work. Here is an example of how a movement session helped Joan to contact her assertiveness.

In this session, Joan described being painfully rejected by a friend, which was totally unexpected. Face to face with her friend, she could only feel her liveliness retreat from consciousness, as if a child had disappeared below the surface of a lake. She had felt herself responding with reasonable understanding to this rejection while emotionally being out of reach. After the incident, which ended pleasantly, she had begun to get glimpses of her anger. As she recounted this at her session we noticed she was guarding her chest rigidly. I suggested she dance out this tension. It was very much like the situation described above (page 98).

She began on her knees in a supplicant motion. Her experience, as she recounted it to me later and not while dancing, was that she had felt a need to implore the mother, "Why have you allowed this to happen?" Instead of mercy, she received stabs to the chest. Unaware of this, I witnessed Joan collapsing onto the floor, seemingly asleep. I wondered whether I should intervene with a question or direction, but decided to trust her body to do what it needed to do. I decided to wait until we were close to the end of the hour before intervening. But after fifteen minutes she sat up and began crawling. The inner process, I learned later, was that she was attacked by the negative mother, who said that she did not deserve love.

Instead of fighting it, Joan decided to give herself up to her fate. She felt herself dragged away, experienced a commotion, and then fell asleep (literally). She woke suddenly when a kind, male voice said, "Hello!" She looked up, surprised at how real the voice seemed, and realized to her astonishment that she had fallen asleep in my office. She was cold and warmed herself by crawling on all fours, during which time she felt in contact with an old, survival-oriented, aggressive part of herself that she called the Tigress (which she had contacted in previous work). With that contact she felt a surge of energy. She stood up and began some very strong swinging motions of her arms and hips, a side-to-side thrusting that finally brought release.

As an introverted feeling type Joan has had to work hard to mobilize aggression and be assertive in relationships. Gradually, through experiencing more of the energy in her back and contacting inner figures like the Tigress, she has changed her capacity to defend herself.

This brief example shows what can happen when body work is combined with traditional analytic therapy. Finding one's own way as a body therapist takes time, experience, willingness to change behavior patterns, and an understanding of one's own typology and resistances.

The Reunion of the Soul and the Body, illustration by William Blake
for Blair's *The Grave* (1808), etched by Schiavonetti.

4

Experiencing the Unus Mundus

The growing movement to incorporate body work into psychotherapy reflects changing attitudes in Western culture, particularly a
new-found awareness of and respect for the feminine principle.

As the collective psyche becomes more accepting of the
feminine, so do magic, mysticism, poetry and artistic sensibilities
come alive in all of us. In the dualism of Western philosophy the
split between spirit and matter separated theology and science, mental and physical, materialism and mysticism in ways that were not
duplicated in the more unified Eastern experience. The female serpent power, the Kundalini, was not buried with the Goddess under
patriarchal cathedrals, but lives within us all and waits patiently for
acknowledgment. Tantric Yoga finds the essence of Godliness in
the union of male and female. Wilhelm Reich seems to have acted
out of the same intuition, but as a typical Western medicine man,
with a strong physical orientation, he did not integrate the spiritual
dimensions into his work.

In the West we have seen the physical sciences split off from
mystery and become almost totally materialistic, while theology
followed a dogmatic path and became progressively devitalized,
less earthy and consequently noninfluential. With Einstein the healing of the schism began to take place in physics. He said: "The
most important function of art and science is to awaken the cosmic
religious feeling and keep it alive."[140] Today geophysicists are
sounding like mystics, awed by the magnitude of the universe and
the earth's ability to produce life and water, maintaining itself at a
viable temperature over eons when variance of a few degrees would
bring annihilation. Quantum physicists find themselves in agreement with the Eastern concept of Prana, the life-energy permeating
the universe.

"Our faith imposes on us a right and duty to throw ourselves into
the things of the earth," says Teilhard de Chardin.[141] Catholic
theologians such as de Chardin and Matthew Fox challenge the

105

notion of original sin and need for redemption as it tends to lead to the degradation of the body. They celebrate the continuance of creation and glorification of God in the material universe, which Fox calls the "original blessing" (as opposed to original sin).

> The fall/redemption model of spirituality, which has dominated theology since the 17th century, is a dualistic model and a patriarchal one; it begins its theology with sin and original sin; and it generally ends with redemption. Fall/redemption spirituality does not teach believers about the New Creation or creativity, about Eros, play, pleasure, and the God of delight. It fails to teach love of the earth or care for the cosmos, and it is so frightened of passion that it fails to listen to the imprisoned pleas of the anawim, the little ones, of human history. This same fear of passion prevents it from helping lovers to celebrate their experiences as spiritual and magical. This tradition has not proven friendly to artists or prophets or Native American peoples or women.[142]
>
> There are either/or choices that we must make—A psychology that says, "The soul makes war with the body" (fall/redemption, Augustine), and one that says, "The soul loves the body" (creation spirituality, Eckhart), are not saying the same thing.[143]

In the Jewish tradition there has been less splitting of matter and spirit. Jewish mysticism, which has always focused on the expression of Godliness in everyday tasks and daily rituals, is now becoming more visible. So are the writings of Catholic mystics such as Meister Eckhart and Hildegard of Bingen. These mystics did not lose touch with the unity of being, did not fall into philosophical dualism. Hildegard wrote:

> The earth is at the same time mother, she is mother of all that is natural, mother of all that is human. She is mother of all, for contained in her are the seeds of all. The earth of humankind contains all moistness, all verdancy, all germinating power. It is in so many ways fruitful. All creation comes from it. Yet it forms not only the basic raw material for humankind, but also the substance of the incarnation of God's son.[144]

With the body recognized as the manifestation of God-energy, the mystic need not retreat to the mountain, but can find the mystical experience in the midst of everyday life. Everyman is an artist, and the world is in a continual process of creation.

Analysts who are used to thinking in terms of mental structures and mental mechanisms of defense will learn to conceptualize in terms of the subtle body and freeing blockages in the somatic unconscious. Their aim will be to create an energy-body of substance which can express the fullest manifestation of Self. Just as we now see psychosomatic processes in physical and mental-emotional images, so will we be able to visualize and sense kinesthetically what is occurring in the body of the analysand, and this will be our automatic and natural response. We will see consciousness fill out spatially within and beyond the physical body as individuation takes place and is expressed in the subtle body or dreambody.

The objective psyche, in this cosmological evolution, has come to recognize the beauty and value of the individual body, resulting in a wave of narcissism whose purpose may be essentially creative. In *Narcissism and Character Transformation,* Schwartz-Salant writes:

> Narcissistic characters may be carrying the seeds of a new conscious experience of the Self in which both matter and spirit, both ascent and descent, have equal value. As such, they would be heralding a change in the collective unconscious Self image.[145]

From this point of view, self-preoccupation reflects the collective need to reunite body and soul.

I believe that the integration of analysis and body therapy contributes to an ongoing universal process of uniting mind, body and soul. I see this integration as offering a way to avoid both the dualism of Cartesian philosophy and the sheer romanticism of Jean Jacques Rousseau, in promoting unity of the psyche.

In Jung's elucidation of the alchemists' work paralleling the individuation process, he describes three stages of the *coniunctio*. The first, the *unio mentalis,* involves the overcoming of the body and realization of the shadow—"the attainment of full knowledge of the heights and depths of one's own character."[146] The second stage is the reunion of the spirit with the body:

> The reuniting of the spiritual position with the body obviously means

that the insights gained should be made real. An insight might just as well remain in abeyance if it is simply not used. The second stage of conjunction therefore consists in making a reality of the man who has acquired some knowledge of his paradoxical wholeness.[147]

The third and final stage of the *coniunctio* is wholeness through transcendence, the *unus mundus,* which psychologically consists in a synthesis of the conscious with the unconscious, the unity of spirit and matter, body and soul.[148]

This is the goal toward which depth psychology and the physical sciences are now moving. As Jung writes:

> Microphysics is feeling its way into the unknown side of matter, just as complex psychology is pushing forward into the unknown side of the psyche. . . . The common background of microphysics and depth-psychology is as much physical as psychic and therefore neither, but rather a third thing, a neutral nature which can at most be grasped in hints since in essence it is transcendental.
>
> The background of our empirical world thus appears to be in fact a *unus mundus.*[149]

While many individuals evolve through the third stage—some becoming mentors and spiritual leaders, others quietly serving in unrecognized and unacknowledged roles—as a collective society I would estimate our human evolution to be overlapping the ending of stage one and beginning of stage two.

Camille Campbell asks in her preface to *Meditations with Teresa of Avila,* "Who will teach us to give birth to our souls, to be life-giving creative centers of energy instead of death-dealing centers of inertia?"[150]

The answer, I believe, is that we shall all teach each other, each carrying some of the flame, each igniting and keeping alive the spark in others and ourselves when we are in danger of falling into the inertia of ungrounded intellectualism or spiritless compulsive physicality. To reach this flame is the point of combining depth analysis and body therapy, for the flame is guarded deeply in the temple of the body.

Notes

CW—*The Collected Works of C.G. Jung*

1. D.H. Lawrence, *St. Mawr and the Man Who Died,* p. 206.
2. C.A. Meier, *Ancient Incubation and Modern Psychotherapy,* pp. 40f.
3. Jung, "On Psychic Energy," *The Structure and Dynamics of the Psyche,* CW 8, par. 47.
4. See, for instance, Marcia Moore and Mark Douglas, *Astrology: The Divine Science,* pp. 685ff.
5. J.L. Halliday, in J.A.C. Brown, *Freud and the Post-Freudians,* p. 99.
6. Ibid., p. 100.
7. Edward C. Whitmont, *Return of the Goddess,* p. 83.
8. Georg Groddeck, *The Book of the It,* p. 227.
9. Ibid., p. 20.
10. Whitmont, *Return of the Goddess,* p. 83.
11. Erich Neumann, *The Origins and History of Consciousness,* p. 290.
12. J.A.C. Brown, *Freud and the Post-Freudians,* p. 66.
13. Groddeck, *The Book of the It,* pp. 196f.
14. Whitmont, "Recent Influences on the Practice of Jungian Analysis," in Murray Stein, ed., *Jungian Analysis,* p. 336.
15. Gerard Lauzun, *Sigmund Freud: The Man and His Theories,* p. 37.
16. Groddeck, *The Book of the It,* p. 238.
17. Lauzun, *Sigmund Freud,* p. 62.
18. Ibid., p. 63.
19. Freud, "'Civilized' Sexual Morality and Modern Nervousness," *Collected Papers,* vol. 2, p. 88.
20. Wilhelm Reich, *The Function of the Orgasm,* p. 130.
21. Lauzun, *Sigmund Freud,* p. 97.
22. Quoted in ibid., p. 98.
23. Freud, "The Libido Theory," *Collected Papers,* vol. 5, p. 132.
24. Ibid., p. 134.
25. Lauzun, *Sigmund Freud,* p. 41.
26. Freud, "Recommendations for Physicians on the Psycho-Analytic Method of Treatment," *Collected Papers,* vol. 2, p. 331.
27. J.A.C. Brown, *Freud and the Post-Freudians,* pp. 51f.
28. William Goodheart, "Successful and Unsuccessful Interventions in

Jungian Analysis: The Construction and Destruction of the Spellbinding Circle," in *Chiron: A Review of Jungian Analysis,* 1984, p. 112.

29. Quoted in Earl Heinz Ansbacher and Rowena Ansbacher, *The Individual Psychology of Alfred Adler,* p. 220.

30. Ibid., p. 222.

31. Ibid., pp. 223f.

32. Liljan Espenak, "The Adlerian Approach in Dance Therapy," in Penny Bernstein, ed., *Eight Theoretical Approaches in Dance Movement,* p. 75.

33. Groddeck, *The Book of the It,* p. 226.

34. Ibid., pp. 28, 24, 14.

35. Reich, *The Function of the Orgasm,* pp. 125ff.

36. Ibid., p. 293.

37. See, for instance, David Boadella, *Wilhelm Reich: The Evolution of His Work.*

38. See P. Trachtman, "The Search for Life's Origins and a First Synthetic Cell," in *Smithsonian,* vol. 15, no. 3 (June 1984), pp. 43ff.

39. Malcolm Brown, "The New Body Psychotherapies."

40. Quoted in Boadella, *Wilhelm Reich,* pp. 369f.

41. Gerda Alexander told me that when Reich was alive she was often asked to work with persons who had been his patients. There were frequently two negative effects of his treatment: 1) it was experienced by some patients as harsh and abusive; and 2) many were unable to resolve their dependence on him, even after years of working with him.

42. Whitmont and Yoram Kaufman, "Analytical Psychology," in Raymond Corsini, ed., *Current Psychotherapies,* pp. 99, 110.

43. Ibid., pp. 110ff.

44. Ibid., p. 111.

45. Ibid., p. 101. Whitmont told me the reference was to breath therapists in Munich. There are still professional organizations of breath therapists in Europe and the United States.

46. See Jung, "On the Nature of the Psyche," *The Structure and Dynamics of the Psyche,* CW 8, pars. 414ff. Jung writes: "It is not only possible but fairly probable, even, that psyche and matter are two different aspects of one and the same thing." (par. 418)

47. See Jung, "The Transcendent Function," ibid., pars. 168ff.

48. Bernstein, *Eight Theoretical Approaches,* p. 5.

49. See Jung, "The Syzygy: Anima and Animus," *Aion,* CW 9ii, pars. 20ff.
50. Bernstein, *Eight Theoretical Approaches,* p. 181.
51. Jung, "The Transcendent Function," *The Structure and Dynamics of the Psyche,* CW 8,
52. Joan Chodorow, "Dance Therapy and the Transcendent Function," in *American Journal of Dance Therapy,* Spring/Summer 1978.
53. Arnold Mindell, *Dreambody: The Body's Role in Revealing the Self,* p. 6.
54. Ibid., p. 7.
55. Nathan Schwartz-Salant, *Narcissism and Character Transformation: The Psychology of Narcissistic Character Disorders,* p. 121.
56. Whitmont and Kaufman, "Analytical Psychology," p. 117.
57. See J.A.C. Brown, *Freud and the Post-Freudians,* pp. 91ff.
58. See Edward W.L. Smith, "The Role of Early Reichian Theory in the Development of Gestalt Psychology," in *Psychotherapy: Theory, Research, and Practice,* vol. 12, no. 3 (Fall 1975).
59. Lecture to Inter-Regional Society of Jungian Analysts, Quebec City, September 1984.
60. Chodorow, "Dance Therapy and the Transcendent Function."
61. Moshe Feldenkrais, *Awareness through Movement: Health Exercises for Personal Growth,* pp. 172f.
62. Mary Starks Whitehouse, "C.G. Jung and Dance Therapy," in Bernstein, *Eight Theoretical Approaches,* p. 51.
63. Sharon Chaiklin and Claire Schmais, "The Chace Approach to Dance Therapy," in ibid., p. 17.
64. Trudi Schoop and Peggy Mitchell, "Reflections and Projections: The Schoop Approach to Dance Therapy," in ibid., pp. 31ff.
65. Marcel Gaumond, "Individuation through Body Awareness: Eutony As Seen by a Jungian Analyst," unpublished manuscript.
66. Gerda Alexander, "Foreword," in ibid.
67. Gaumond, ibid.
68. Anita Greene, "Giving the Body Its Due," *Quadrant,* Fall 1984, p. 15.
69. Ibid., pp. 9ff.
70. See Chodorow, "Dance Movement and Body Experience in Analysis," in Stein, *Jungian Analysis,* and "To Move and Be Moved," in *Quadrant,* Fall 1984.
71. Malcolm Brown, "The New Body Psychotherapies."

72. Malcolm Brown, *The Healing Touch: Introduction to Organismic Psycho-Therapy,* pp. xiv-xv.

73. Ibid.

74. Ibid.

75. Malcolm Brown, "Organismic Psychotherapy."

76. Albert Pesso, personal communication.

77. Mindell, *Dreambody,* p. 199.

78. Ibid., p. 197.

79. Ibid., p. 8.

80. Marion Woodman, personal communication.

81. See *The Owl Was a Baker's Daughter: Obesity, Anorexia Nervosa and the Repressed Feminine* and *Addiction to Perfection: The Still Unravished Bride.*

82. Whitmont, "Recent Influences," p. 347.

83. See Jung, "The Psychology of the Unconscious," *The Practice of Psychotherapy,* CW 16, par. 381.

84. Schwartz-Salant, *Narcissism,* p. 25.

85. Harriet Machtiger, "Reflections on the Transference/Counter-transference Process with Borderline Patients," in *Chiron* 1984, p. 138.

86. See Goodheart, "Successful and Unsuccessful Interventions in Jungian Analysis: The Construction and Destruction of the Spellbinding Circle," in *Chiron* 1984, and "Theory of Analytic Interaction: Review of Writings by Robert Langs and Harold Searles," in *San Francisco Jung Foundation Library Journal,* vol. 4, no. 4 (1980).

87. See Joseph Masterson, *Countertransference and Psychotherapeutic Technique.*

88. Goodheart, "Successful and Unsuccessful Interactions," p. 99.

89. Mindell, *Dreambody.*

90. Whitmont, "Recent Influences."

91. Florence Wiedemann, "Mother, Father, Teacher, Sister: Transference/Countertransference Issues with Women in the First Stage of Animus Development," in *Chiron* 1984, p. 182.

92. Ibid., p. 187.

93. Woodman, personal communication.

94. Goodheart, "Theory of Analytic Interaction."

95. Ibid.

96. Ibid.

97. Schwartz-Salant, *Narcissism,* p. 107.

98. Ibid., p. 155.

99. Chodorow, "Dance Movement and Body Experience in Analysis," p. 200.
100. Greene, "Giving the Body Its Due," p. 16.
101. See Schwartz-Salant, *Narcissism,* pp. 111f.
102. Goodheart, "Successful and Unsuccessful Interventions," p. 109.
103. D.W. Winnicott, *The Child and the Outside World,* p. 5.
104. Greene, "Giving the Body Its Due," p. 11. The remark by Jung is from "The Psychology of Dementia Praecox," *The Psychogenesis of Mental Disease,* CW 3, par. 90.
105. Woodman, "Psyche/Soma Awareness," in *Quadrant,* Fall 1984, p. 28.
106. Malcolm Brown, "Organismic Psychotherapy."
107. Goodheart, "Successful and Unsuccessful Interventions," p. 110.
108. Jung, *Psychological Types,* CW 6, pars. 88ff.
109. Whitmont, "Recent Influences," p. 354.
110. Greene, "Giving the Body Its Due," pp. 10f.
111. Woodman, "Psyche/Soma Awareness," pp. 26ff.
112. In *Chiron,* 1984. See also Mario Jacoby, *The Analytic Encounter: Transference and Human Relationship,* chapter 7, "Erotic Love in Analysis."
113. Schwartz-Salant, "Archetypal Factors Underlying Sexual Acting-Out in the Transference/Countertransference Process," in *Chiron* 1984, p. 29.
114. Ibid.
115. Jung, *The Practice of Psychotherapy,* CW 16, pars. 422ff.
116. Whitmont, "Recent Influences," p. 342.
117. Schwartz-Salant, "Archetypal Factors Underlying Sexual Acting-Out," pp. 29, 20.
118. Whitmont, "Recent Influences," p. 354.
119. Jacoby, *The Analytic Encounter.*
120. Jung, "The Psychology of the Transference," *The Practice of Psychotherapy,* CW 16, par. 448.
121. Masterson, *Countertransference and Psychotherapeutic Techniques.*
122. Chodorow, "Dance Movement and Body Experience in Analysis," p. 199.
123. Whitmont, "Recent Influences," p. 342.
124. In *Alchemical Studies,* CW 13 (originally published in Richard Wilhelm, *The Secret of the Golden Flower*).
125. Schwartz-Salant, *Narcissism,* p. 93.
126. Jung, *Memories, Dreams, Reflections,* p. 177.

127. Gaumond, "Individuation through Body Awareness."
128. O. Carl Simonton and Stephanie Simonton, *Getting Well Again.*
129. See, for instance, *Collected Papers of Milton H. Erickson on Hypnosis.*
130. Malcolm Brown, *The Healing Touch.*
131. Goodheart, "Successful and Unsuccessful Interventions," p. 107.
132. Greene, "Giving the Body Its Due," p. 17.
133. The variety of approaches to Jungian training is discussed in Stein, *Jungian Analysis,* pp. 367ff.
134. Chodorow, "The Body as Symbol: Dance Movement in Analysis."
135. Mindell, *Dreambody,* p. 3.
136. See Jung, "General Description of the Types," *Psychological Types,* CW 6, pars. 536ff.
137. Jung, "A Contribution to the Study of Psychological Types," ibid., par. 882. In this essay Jung was paticularly concerned with the differences between the psychologies of Freud and Adler.
138. Greene, "Giving the Body Its Due," p. 10.
139. Woodman, "Psyche/Soma Awareness," p. 29.
140. Quoted in Matthew Fox, *Original Blessing,* p. 66.
141. Ibid., p. 59.
142. Ibid., p. 11.
143. Ibid., p. 28.
144. Ibid., p. 65.
145. Schwartz-Salant, *Narcissism,* p. 70.
146. Jung, *Mysterium Coniunctionis,* CW 14, par. 674.
147. Ibid., par. 679.
148. Ibid., par. 770.
149. Ibid., pars. 768f.
150. Camille Campbell, *Meditations with Teresa of Avila,* p. 5.

Glossary of Jungian Terms

Anima (Latin, "soul"). The unconscious, feminine side of a man's personality. She is personified in dreams by images of women ranging from prostitute and seductress to spiritual guide (Wisdom). She is the eros principle, hence a man's anima development is reflected in how he relates to women. Identification with the anima can appear as moodiness, effeminacy, and oversensitivity. Jung calls the anima *the archetype of life itself.*

Animus (Latin, "spirit"). The unconscious, masculine side of a woman's personality. He personifies the logos principle. Identification with the animus can cause a woman to become rigid, opinionated, and argumentative. More positively, he is the inner man who acts as a bridge between the woman's ego and her own creative resources in the unconscious.

Archetypes. Irrepresentable in themselves, but their effects appear in consciousness as the archetypal images and ideas. These are universal patterns or motifs which come from the collective unconscious and are the basic content of religions, mythologies, legends, and fairytales.

Association. A spontaneous flow of interconnected thoughts and images around a specific idea, determined by unconscious connections.

Complex. An emotionally charged group of ideas or images. At the "center" of a complex is an archetype or archetypal image.

Constellate. Whenever there is a strong emotional reaction to a person or a situation, a complex has been constellated (activated).

Ego. The central complex in the field of consciousness. A strong ego can relate objectively to activated contents of the unconscious (i.e., other complexes), rather than identifying with them, which appears as a state of possession.

Feeling. One of the four psychic functions. It is a rational function which evaluates the worth of relationships and situations. Feeling must be distinguished from emotion, which is due to an activated complex.

115

Individuation. The conscious realization of one's unique psychological reality, including both strengths and limitations. It leads to the experience of the Self as the regulating center of the psyche.

Inflation. A state in which one has an unrealistically high or low (negative inflation) sense of identity.

Intuition. One of the four psychic functions. It is the irrational function which tells us the possibilities inherent in the present. In contrast to **sensation** (the function which perceives immediate reality through the physical senses) intuition perceives via the unconscious, e.g., flashes of insight of unknown origin.

Persona (Latin, "actor's mask"). One's social role, derived from the expectations of society and early training.

Projection. The process whereby an unconscious quality or characteristic of one's own is perceived and reacted to in an outer object or person.

Self. The archetype of wholeness and the regulating center of the personality. It is experienced as a transpersonal power which transcends the ego, e.g., God.

Shadow. An unconscious part of the personality characterized by traits and attitudes, whether negative or positive, which the conscious ego tends to reject or ignore. It is personified in dreams by persons of the same sex as the dreamer.

Symbol. The best possible expression for something essentially unknown. Symbolic thinking is non-linear, right-brain oriented; it is complementary to logical, linear, left-brain thinking.

Transcendent function. The reconciling "third" which emerges from the unconscious (in the form of a symbol or a new attitude) after the conflicting opposites have been made conscious and held in awareness.

Transference-countertransference. Particular cases of projection, commonly used to describe the unconscious, emotional bonds that arise between two persons in a therapeutic relationship.

Unus Mundus. The third stage of the alchemical *coniunctio,* corresponding to psychological wholeness, a state in which ego-consciousness and the unconscious work together in harmony.

Bibliography

Ansbacher, Earl Heinz, and Ansbacher, Rowena. *The Individual Psychology of Alfred Adler*. New York: Basic Books, 1956.

Bernstein, Penny, ed. *Eight Theoretical Approaches in Dance Movement*. Dubuque, Iowa: Kendall-Hunt Publishing Co., 1979.

Boadella, David. *Wilhelm Reich: The Evolution of His Work*. New York: Dell Publishing Co., 1971.

Bolen, Jean Shinoda. *Goddesses in Every Woman*. New York: Harper and Row, 1984.

Brown, J.A.C. *Freud and the Post-Freudians*. Baltimore: Penguin Books, 1961.

Brown, Malcolm. *The Healing Touch: An Introduction to Organismic Psycho-Therapy*. Privately published, 1985.

————. "Organismic Psychotherapy." Lecture, Warrenton, Virginia, February 9, 1985.

————. "The New Body Psychotherapies." Unpublished manuscript, 1974.

Campbell, Camille. *Meditations with Teresa of Avila*. Santa Fe: Bear and Co., 1985.

Chaiklin, Sharon, and Schmais, Claire. "The Chace Approach to Dance Therapy." In *Eight Theoretical Approaches in Dance Movement*. Ed. Penny Bernstein. Dubuque, Iowa: Kendall-Hunt Publishing Co., 1979.

Chodorow, Joan. "Dance Movement and Body Experience in Analysis." In *Jungian Analysis*. Ed. Murray Stein. Boulder: Shambhala Publications, 1982.

————. "Dance Therapy and the Transcendent Function." In *American Journal of Dance Therapy*, Spring/Summer 1978.

————. "To Move and Be Moved." In *Quadrant: Journal of the C.G. Jung Foundation for Analytical Psychology*, vol. 17, no. 2 (Fall 1984).

————. "The Body as Symbol: Dance Movement in Analysis." Paper given at Ghost Ranch Conference, 1985.

Corsini, Raymond, ed. *Current Psychotherapies*. Itasca, Illinois: F.E. Peacock Publishing Co., 1973.

Erickson, Milton H. *Collected Papers of Milton H. Erickson on Hypnosis*. New York: Irvington Press, 1980.

Espenak, Liljan. "The Adlerian Approach in Dance Therapy." In *Eight Theoretical Approaches in Dance Movement*. Ed. Penny Bernstein. Dubuque, Iowa: Kendall-Hunt Publishing Co., 1979.

Feldenkrais, Moshe. *Awareness through Movement: Health Exercises for Personal Growth*. New York: Harper and Row, 1972.

Fox, Matthew. *Original Blessing*. Santa Fe: Bear and Co., 1983.

Freud, Sigmund. *Collected Papers*. 6 vols. New York: Basic Books, 1959.

Gaumond, Marcel. "Individuation through Body Awareness: Eutony As Seen by a Jungian Analyst." Unpublished manuscript.

Goodheart, William B. "Theory of Analytic Interaction: Review of Writings by Robert Langs and Harold Searles." *San Francisco Jung Foundation Library Journal*, vol. 4, no. 4 (1980).

————. "Successful and Unsuccessful Interventions in Jungian Analysis: The Construction and Destruction of the Spellbinding Circle." In *Chiron: A Review of Jungian Analysis*. Wilmette, Illinois: Chiron Publications, 1984.

Greene, Anita. "Giving the Body Its Due." In *Quadrant: Journal of the C.G. Jung Foundation for Analytical Psychology*, vol. 17, no. 2 (Fall 1984).

Groddeck, Georg. *The Book of the It*. New York: The New American Library of World Literature, 1961.

Jacoby, Mario. *The Analytic Encounter: Transference and Human Relationship*. Toronto: Inner City Books, 1984.

Jung, C.G. *The Collected Works* (Bollingen Series XX). 20 vols. Trans. R.F.C. Hull. Ed. H. Read, M. Fordham, G. Adler, Wm. McGuire. Princeton: Princeton University Press, 1953-1979.

————. *Memories, Dreams, Reflections*. Trans. Richard and Clara Winston. Ed. Aniela Jaffé. New York: Pantheon Books, 1963.

Lauzun, Gerard. *Sigmund Freud: The Man and His Theories*. Greenwich, Connecticut: Fawcett Publishing, Inc., 1965.

Lawrence, D.H. *St. Mawr and the Man Who Died*. New York: Vintage Books, 1953.

Machtiger, Harriet Gordon. "Reflections on the Transference/Countertransference Process with Borderline Patients." In *Chiron: A Review of Jungian Analysis*. Wilmette, Illinois: Chiron Publications, 1984.

Masterson, Joseph. *Countertransference and Psychotherapeutic Techniques*. New York: Bruner Mazell, 1983.

Meier, C.A. *Ancient Incubation and Modern Psychotherapy*. Evanston: Northwestern University Press, 1967.

Mindell, Arnold. *Dreambody: The Body's Role in Revealing the Self*. Santa Monica: Sigo Press, 1982.

Moore, Marcia, and Douglas, Mark. *Astrology: The Divine Science*. York Harbor, Maine: Arcane Publications, 1971.

Neumann, Eric. *The Origins and History of Consciousness* (Bollingen Series XLII). Trans. R.F.C. Hull. Princeton University Press, Princeton, 1970.

Perera, Sylvia Brinton. *Descent to the Goddess*. Toronto: Inner City Books, 1981.

Reich, Wilhelm. *The Function of the Orgasm*. New York: Farrar, Straus, and Giroux, 1942.

Samuels, Andrew. *Jung and the Post-Jungians*. London: Routledge and Kegan Paul, 1985.

Schoop, Trudi, and Mitchell, Peggy. "Reflections and Projections: The Schoop Approach to Dance Therapy." In *Eight Theoretical Approaches in Dance Movement*. Ed. Penny Bernstein. Dubuque, Iowa: Kendall-Hunt Publishing Co., 1979.

Schwartz-Salant, Nathan. "Archetypal Factors Underlying Sexual Acting-Out in the Transference/Countertransference Process." In *Chiron: A Review of Jungian Analysis*. Wilmette, Illinois: Chiron Publications, 1984.

―――――. *Narcissism and Character Transformation: The Psychology of Narcissistic Character Disorders*. Toronto: Inner City Books, 1982.

Simonton, O. Carl, and Simonton, Stephanie. *Getting Well Again*. Los Angeles: Cancer Control Society, 1978.

Smith, Edward W.L. "The Role of Early Reichian Theory in the Development of Gestalt Psychology." In *Psychotherapy: Theory, Research, and Practice*, vol. 12, no. 3 (Fall 1975).

Stein, Murray, ed. *Jungian Analysis*. Boulder: Shambhala Publications, 1982.

Trachtman, P. "The Search for Life's Origins and a First Synthetic Cell." In *Smithsonian*, vol. 15, no. 3 (June 1984).

Whitehouse, Mary Starks. "C.G. Jung and Dance Therapy." In *Eight Theoretical Approaches in Dance Movement*. Ed. Penny Bernstein. Dubuque, Iowa: Kendall-Hunt Publishing Co., 1979.

Whitmont, Edward C. "Recent Influences on the Practice of Jungian Analysis." In *Jungian Analysis*. Ed. Murray Stein. Boulder: Shambhala Publications, 1982.

―――――. *Return of the Goddess*. New York: Crossroad Publishing Co., 1982.

Whitmont, Edward C., and Kaufman, Yoram. "Analytical Psychology." In *Current Psychotherapies*. Ed. Raymond Corsini. Itasca, Illinois: F.E. Peacock Publishing Co., 1973.

Wiedemann, Florence. "Mother, Father, Teacher, Sister: Transference/ Countertransference Issues with Women in the First Stage of Animus Development." In *Chiron: A Review of Jungian Analysis*. Wilmette, Illinois: Chiron Publications, 1984.

Wilhelm, Richard. *The Secret of the Golden Flower*. New York: Harcourt, Brace and World, 1931.

Winnicott, D.W. *The Child and the Outside World*. London: Tavistock Publishers, 1957.

Woodman, Marion. *Addiction to Perfection: The Still Unravished Bride*. Toronto: Inner City Books, 1982.

———. *The Owl Was a Baker's Daughter: Obesity, Anorexia Nervosa and the Repressed Feminine*. Toronto: Inner City Books, 1980.

———. "Psyche/Soma Awareness." In *Quadrant: Journal of the C.G. Jung Foundation for Analytical Psychology,* vol. 17, no. 2 (Fall 1984).

———. *The Pregnant Virgin: A Process of Psychological Transformation*. Toronto: Inner City Books, 1985.

Index

abreaction, 15
active imagination, 11-12, 40, 44, 56,
    58, 63, 66, 97
Adler, Alfred, 27, 29, 32-35, 73
aerobics, 14
affect (*see also* emotion), 16-17, 81-86
Age of Reason, 12
aggression, 29-30, 34, 36, 103
alchemy, alchemists, 42, 107-108,
    116
alcoholism, 68
Alexander, Franz, 43, 101
Alexander, Frederick Matthias, 45-46,
    48, 50, 67
Alexander, Gerda, 45, 48, 67, 83, 94,
    101
Analytic Encounter, The, 78
anger, 92-93
anima, 39-41, 115
animus, 39-41, 63, 88, 115
"Anna O.," 15
Apollo, 10-11
Apollonian, 27
archetype(s), archetypal, 11-13, 18,
    20, 41-42, 64, 68-70, 77, 95,
    115
"Archetypal Factors Underlying
    Sexual Acting-Out," 74
armoring, 35-36, 51-54, 66-68, 71-73,
    79-80, 96
Assagioli, 40
association, *see* free association
astrology, 21
Augustine, St., 106

Bach, 42
Bartenieff, Irmgard, 46
behavioral therapy, 81, 84-85, 96
Bernstein, Penny, 40
Big Sur, 50

bioenergetics, 38, 50-52, 82, 96
biofeedback, 13, 42, 56, 81-82, 85
black hole, 87-92
Blake, William, 104
Bleuler, 24
body: armor, 35-36, 51-54, 66-68, 71-
    73, 79-80, 96
  as feminine, 24-26
  processes, 91-92
  and psyche, 42, 85-86, 110
  and Self, 25
  subtle, 56, 76, 107
body ego, 31
body therapy: cultural background, 21-
    27
  and dance movement, 44-51
  defined, 13-14
  Jung's influence, 38-43
  pioneers, 27-43
Bolen, Jean Shinoda, 26
borderline disorders, 81
Bosanquet, Camilla, 73-74
breath, breathing, 40, 57, 82, 88, 98
Breuer, 15, 69
"brief" therapies, 45
Brown, J.A.C., 26
Brown, Malcolm, 37, 51-54, 71-72,
    85, 101
Brucke, 15

Campbell, Camille, 108
cancer, 84
catharsis, 82, 84
celibacy, 70
Chace, Marion, 47
Character Analysis, 38, 81
character armor, *see* armoring
Charcot, 15
childbearing, 22-23
Chiron, 11

chiropractic, 11
Chodorow, Joan, 41, 46, 51, 68, 81,
    94
Christ, 9
collective unconscious, 19, 36, 60
"Commentary on *The Secret of the
    Golden Flower*," 82
compensation, 33, 70-71
complexes, 11-14, 16-20, 40, 51, 69-
    74, 80-93, 95, 115
conflict, 17-19, 44
coniunctio, 76-77, 107-108, 116
constellate, 115
countertransference, 32, 59, 63, 66,
    75-80, 116
*Countertransference and
    Psychotherapeutic Techniques*,
    80-81

dance movement, 21, 34, 39-40, 44-
    58, 61, 96-98, 100-103
dearmoring, 67-68
death instinct, 29-30
dependency, 33
depression, 19, 65
Descartes, 12, 24
Descent to the Goddess, 26
Dexion, 11
dreams, 11-12, 40-42, 58, 62-63, 65-
    67, 78-79, 86-93, 98-99
dreambody, 56-57, 98, 101, 107
Dreambody, 42, 55-56
drive theory, 27-31
dualism, 12-13, 23, 62, 105-107
Duncan, Isadora, 45

eating disorders, 57
Effort/Shape, 46
ego: and body, 31, 41, 71-74
    and complexes, 17-20, 67, 115
    inner-determined, 81
    and libido, 31
    and Self, 11-14, 63, 82
    and superego, 30

"Ego and the Id, The," 30
Einstein, Albert, 105
emotion: 16-17, 34-35, 65-67, 81-86
    "negative," 92-93
enactment, 58
enantiodromia, 9
energy, psychic: 16-17, 20, 27-34, 39-
    40, 42, 51-54
    repressed, 72-75
Enlightenment, 12
Ennis, Katherine, 53
envy, 92-93
Erickson, Milton, 84-85
Eros, 9-10, 29
Esalen, 44
Espanek, Liljan, 34
Eutony, 48-49, 83
existentialism, 21
extraversion, 99-102

faith healing, 14
fall/redemption, 106
Fay, Carolyn Grant, 51, 57
fear, 92-93
feeling function, 41, 82, 99-103, 115
Feldenkrais, Moshe, 14, 44, 46-48,
    50, 67
feminine, 9-10, 21-26, 60, 64, 88-93,
    95-96, 105-107
Ferenczi, Sandor, 27, 32-33, 35-36,
    44
fields, interactional, 63-64
fingers, 10-11
Fox, Matthew, 105-106
frame, analytic, 59, 62-64
free association, 16, 28, 31
Freud, Sigmund, 15-16, 18-19, 22,
    24, 27-38, 69, 73
Freud and the Post-Freudians, 26

Gaumond, Marcel, 48-49, 83
gestalt therapy, 40, 50, 56, 58
Ghost Ranch Conference, 94, 97

Goddesses in Every Woman, 26
Goodheart, William, 32, 62-64, 70, 72, 95
gratification: 61, 67-76, 96
  of analyst's needs, 75-76
  through embodiment, 70-72
  individual differences, 72-73
  of patient's needs, 73-74
  symbolic, 69-70
Great Mother, 18-19, 55, 73
Greene, Anita, 50-51, 68, 71, 73-74, 94-95, 100-101
Groddeck, George, 24, 26, 27-30, 34-35
group therapy, 21, 39, 43-45, 57-58

Halliday, J.L., 22, 54
hands, 10-11
Harlow, Harry, 23
Hatha Yoga, 21, 56, 82-83
"here and now," 44
Hildegard of Bingen, 106
Hinduism, 21
hole in earth, 87-92
holistic medicine, 21, 34
homosexuality, 25-26, 75
hypnosis, 15-16, 23, 28
hysteria, 15, 22

Id, 30
identification, with complex, 17-18
illness, psychosomatic, 12, 22
impotence, 36
individuation, 11, 38, 48-49, 56, 59-60, 69-70, 78, 81, 107, 116
inflation, 61, 98, 116
instinct, 12-14, 61, 69
introversion, 80, 99-101
intuition, 53, 80, 97, 116
Isis, 9
"It," 24, 28, 34

Jacoby, Mario, 78
Janov, Arthur, 50-51, 81

jealousy, 92-93
Joan (analysand), 97-98, 102-103
Jung, C.G., 9, 16-20, 22, 24-25, 29-30, 36, 38-44, 49, 53, 55, 58-59, 69, 73, 76, 78, 80-82, 85, 99-100, 107-108
Jung, Emma, 101
Jung and the Post-Jungians, 63

Kaufmann, Yoram, 39-40
Keleman, Stanley, 50
kinship libido, 75-76
Krafft-Ebing, 27
Kundalini, 24-25, 41-42, 56, 105

Labananalysis, 46
Lamb, Warren, 46
Langs, Robert, 63
Lauzun, Gerard, 28, 31
Lawrence, D.H., 9
Lee (analysand), 65-67, 73, 78-80, 86-93, 97-98, 102
libido *(see also* energy, psychic), 29-37, 39, 75, 80
"Libido Theory," 30
Lockhart, Russell, 42
Logos, 9
Lowen, Alexander, 38, 50-52

Machtiger, Harriet, 59-60
Malinowksi, 23
mandala, 41
masculine, 22-23, 25-26, 65, 88
massage, 14, 36, 50, 78-79
Masterson, Joseph, 80-81
matriarchy, 9, 23
Mead, Margaret, 23
meditation, 82, 85-86
Meditations with Teresa of Avila, 108
Meier, C.A., 10, 42
Meister Eckhart, 106
Mindell, Arnold, 40, 42, 51, 55-57, 63, 67, 93-94, 98, 101
mirroring, 67-68

Moreno, Jacob, 43-44, 58
mother complex, 18-19, 86-93, 97-98
movement, *see* dance movement
muscular armor (*see also* armoring),
    36-38, 51, 71
mysticism, 36, 39, 105-107

narcissism, 30-31, 81, 107
*Narcissism and Character
    Transformation,* 107
Neumann, Erich, 25
neurosis, 15, 25, 30, 81
Nietzsche, Friedrich, 24, 27, 30
North, Marion, 46
numinous, 39, 91, 100

"organ dialect," 33
orgasm theory, 36-38
orgone energy, 37
Orgonomy Association, 50, 94
*Origins and History of Consciousness,
    The,* 25

paranoia, 30
patriarchy, patriarchal, 22-23, 25-27,
    60, 81, 95-96, 105-106
Perera, Sylvia Brinton, 26
Perls, Fritz, 40, 44, 50-51, 58
Perriakos, John, 50
persona, 63-64, 71, 116
Pesso, Albert, 51, 55, 101
physics, 101, 105, 108
Plato, 12
posture, 17, 24, 33-34, 44-46
Prana, 105
pregnancy, 17-18, 102-103
Primal Therapy, 50-51
projection, 17-18, 39, 116
proprioception, 40-41, 63, 101
psyche, and body, 42, 85-86, 110
psychodrama, 32, 43-44, 55-56, 58
psychoid, 13
"Psychology of the Transference," 76

psychosomatic medicine, 22, 34-35,
    38
Psychosomatic Medicine, 43

rage, 82-84
Raknes, Ola, 53
Redfearn, 42
regression, 39, 71-72
Reich, Wilhelm, 16, 22, 29, 31, 34-
    38, 44, 48, 51-53, 68, 81, 85,
    105
relaxation, *see* meditation
repression, 15-16, 19, 22, 32, 70, 74
res cogitans, 12
res extensa, 12
Return of the Goddess, 26
Ribble, Margaret, 23
Rolf, Ida, 44, 50
Romantics, 12
Rousseau, Jean-Jacques, 12, 24, 107
Rubenfeld, Ilana, 50-51

Samuels, Andrew, 63
sandplay, 64
Schelling, 12
Schiller, 27
schizophrenia, 30, 42
Schoop, Trudi, 48, 51
Schwartz-Salant, Nathan, 42, 59, 64,
    74-77, 82, 107
Searles, Harold, 63
Self: and body, 25, 107
    and ego, 11-14, 63, 82
    as regulating center, 47, 69, 72,
        116
    split-off, 64
sensation function, 41, 61, 82, 99-
    102, 116
sensitivity training, 9, 40, 43
sex, sexuality, 28-32, 35-39, 48, 54,
    65, 67, 70-80, 89-93, 95-97

shadow, 26, 39, 67, 74, 82, 86, 95-97, 116
Shekinah, 25
Simonton, Carl and Stephanie, 84
"skin talk," 42
somatic unconscious, *see* dream body *and* subtle body
somatization, 12
spirit, embodied, 9, 19, 82, 104, 107-108
Spitz, Rene, 23
Structural Integration, 50
subtle body (*see also* dreambody), 56, 76, 107
superego, 30-31
symbol, 20, 42, 116
symbolic approach, 32-33, 62-63, 69-73
synchronicity, 42, 68

Tai Chi Ch'uan, 14
Tantra Yoga, 105
Teilhard de Chardin, 105
temenos, 69, 95
tension, 17, 22, 33-34, 36, 41, 66, 68, 70, 72, 85, 97-98, 102-103
Thanatos, 29
thinking function, 99-103
touch: 13-14, 51, 62-86
    and analytic model, 62-67
    and analytic training, 93-97
    and contact, 49
    and gratification, 67-76
    meaning of, 67-68
    resistance to, 26, 60-62
    taboo against, 10
    und timing, 80-86
    and transference, 59, 62-66, 74, 76-80
    and typology, 99-103

training, 76, 93-97
transcendence, 108
transcendent function, 41, 64, 69, 116
transference, 14, 30, 32, 38, 51, 59, 61, 63-64, 66, 74-80, 94-95, 116
transformation, 12, 14, 17, 20, 42, 58-59, 69
typology, 39-41, 61, 99-103

unity, psychic, 23, 107-108
unus mundus, 107-108, 116

vegetotherapy, 36, 38
Victorianism, 21-22
visions, 41
Von Laban, Rudolph, 46

Waal, Nic, 37-38
Whitehouse, Mary Starks, 47, 51, 57
Whitmont, Edward C., 23, 25-26, 39-40, 43, 51, 58, 63, 67, 73, 76-78
Wiedemann, Florence, 63
Winnicott, D.W., 71
Woodman, Marion, 51, 57, 63, 71, 73-74, 94, 101
Word Association Test, 16-17, 24, 41-42
wounded healer, 68
wounding, in infancy, 71-73

Yin/Yang, 79
yoga, 21, 56, 82-83, 85, 104

Zen Buddhism, 21, 56
Zeus, 10-11
Ziegler, 42

Studies in Jungian Psychology
by Jungian Analysts

Quality Paperbacks

Prices and payment in $US (except in Canada, $Cdn)

1. The Secret Raven: Conflict and Transformation
Daryl Sharp (Toronto). ISBN 0-919123-00-7. 128 pp. $16

2. The Psychological Meaning of Redemption Motifs in Fairy Tales
Marie-Louise von Franz (Zürich). ISBN 0-919123-01-5. 128 pp. $16

3. On Divination and Synchronicity: The Psychology of Meaningful Chance
Marie-Louise von Franz (Zürich). ISBN 0-919123-02-3. 128 pp. $16

4. The Owl Was a Baker's Daughter: Obesity, Anorexia and the Repressed Feminine Marion Woodman (Toronto). ISBN 0-919123-03-1. 144 pp. $16

5. Alchemy: An Introduction to the Symbolism and the Psychology
Marie-Louise von Franz (Zürich). ISBN 0-919123-04-X. 288 pp. $20

6. Descent to the Goddess: A Way of Initiation for Women
Sylvia Brinton Perera (New York). ISBN 0-919123-05-8. 112 pp. $16

7. The Psyche as Sacrament: A Comparative Study of C.G. Jung and Paul Tillich John P. Dourley (Ottawa). ISBN 0-919123-06-6. 128 pp. $16

8. Border Crossings: Carlos Castaneda's Path of Knowledge
Donald Lee Williams (Boulder). ISBN 0-919123-07-4. 160 pp. $16

9. Narcissism and Character Transformation: The Psychology of Narcissistic Character Disorders
Nathan Schwartz-Salant (New York). ISBN 0-919123-08-2. 192 pp. $18

10. Rape and Ritual: A Psychological Study
Bradley A. Te Paske (Santa Barbara). ISBN 0-919123-09-0. 160 pp. $16

11. Alcoholism and Women: The Background and the Psychology
Jan Bauer (Montreal). ISBN 0-919123-10-4. 144 pp. $16

12. Addiction to Perfection: The Still Unravished Bride
Marion Woodman (Toronto). ISBN 0-919123-11-2. 208 pp. $18pb/$25hc

13. Jungian Dream Interpretation: A Handbook of Theory and Practice
James A. Hall, M.D. (Dallas). ISBN 0-919123-12-0. 128 pp. $16

14. The Creation of Consciousness: Jung's Myth for Modern Man
Edward F. Edinger (Los Angeles). ISBN 0-919123-13-9. 128 pp. $16

15. The Analytic Encounter: Transference and Human Relationship
Mario Jacoby (Zürich). ISBN 0-919123-14-7. 128 pp. $16

16. Change of Life: Dreams and the Menopause
Ann Mankowitz (Ireland). ISBN 0-919123-15-5. 128 pp. $16

17. The Illness That We Are: A Jungian Critique of Christianity
John P. Dourley (Ottawa). ISBN 0-919123-16-3. 128 pp. $16

18. Hags and Heroes: A Feminist Approach to Jungian Psychotherapy with Couples Polly Young-Eisendrath (Philadelphia). ISBN 0-919123-17-1. 192 pp. $18

19. Cultural Attitudes in Psychological Perspective
Joseph L. Henderson, M.D. (San Francisco). ISBN 0-919123-18-X. 128 pp. $16

20. The Vertical Labyrinth: Individuation in Jungian Psychology
Aldo Carotenuto (Rome). ISBN 0-919123-19-8. 144 pp. $16

21. The Pregnant Virgin: A Process of Psychological Transformation
Marion Woodman (Toronto). ISBN 0-919123-20-1. 208 pp. $18pb/$25hc

22. Encounter with the Self: A Jungian Commentary on William Blake's
Illustrations of the Book of Job
Edward F. Edinger (Los Angeles). ISBN 0-919123-21-X. 80 pp. $15

23. The Scapegoat Complex: Toward a Mythology of Shadow and Guilt
Sylvia Brinton Perera (New York). ISBN 0-919123-22-8. 128 pp. $16

24. The Bible and the Psyche: Individuation Symbolism in the Old Testament
Edward F. Edinger (Los Angeles). ISBN 0-919123-23-6. 176 pp. $18

25. The Spiral Way: A Woman's Healing Journey
Aldo Carotenuto (Rome). ISBN 0-919123-24-4. 144 pp. $16

26. The Jungian Experience: Analysis and Individuation
James A. Hall, M.D. (Dallas). ISBN 0-919123-25-2. 176 pp. $18

27. Phallos: Sacred Image of the Masculine
Eugene Monick (Scranton, PA). ISBN 0-919123-26-0. 144 pp. $16

28. The Christian Archetype: A Jungian Commentary on the Life of Christ
Edward F. Edinger (Los Angeles). ISBN 0-919123-27-9. 144 pp. $16

29. Love, Celibacy and the Inner Marriage
John P. Dourley (Ottawa). ISBN 0-919123-28-7. 128 pp. $16

30. Touching: Body Therapy and Depth Psychology
Deldon Anne McNeely (Lynchburg, VA). ISBN 0-919123-29-5. 128 pp. $16

31. Personality Types: Jung's Model of Typology
Daryl Sharp (Toronto). ISBN 0-919123-30-9. 128 pp. $16

32. The Sacred Prostitute: Eternal Aspect of the Feminine
Nancy Qualls-Corbett (Birmingham). ISBN 0-919123-31-7. 176 pp. $18

33. When the Spirits Come Back
Janet O. Dallett (Seal Harbor, WA). ISBN 0-919123-32-5. 160 pp. $16

34. The Mother: Archetypal Image in Fairy Tales
Sibylle Birkhäuser-Oeri (Zürich). ISBN 0-919123-33-3. 176 pp. $18

35. The Survival Papers: Anatomy of a Midlife Crisis
Daryl Sharp (Toronto). ISBN 0-919123-34-1. 160 pp. $16

36. The Cassandra Complex: Living with Disbelief
Laurie Layton Schapira (New York). ISBN 0-919123-35-X. 160 pp. $16

37. Dear Gladys: The Survival Papers, Book 2
Daryl Sharp (Toronto). ISBN 0-919123-36-8. 144 pp. $16

38. The Phallic Quest: Priapus and Masculine Inflation
James Wyly (Chicago). ISBN 0-919123-37-6. 128 pp. $16

39. Acrobats of the Gods: Dance and Transformation
Joan Dexter Blackmer (Wilmot Flat, NH). ISBN 0-919123-38-4. 128 pp. $16

40. Eros and Pathos: Shades of Love and Suffering
Aldo Carotenuto (Rome). ISBN 0-919123-39-2. 160 pp. $16

41. The Ravaged Bridegroom: Masculinity in Women
Marion Woodman (Toronto). ISBN 0-919123-42-2. 224 pp. $20

43. Goethe's *Faust:* Notes for a Jungian Commentary
Edward F. Edinger (Los Angeles). ISBN 0-919123-44-9. 112 pp. $18

44. The Dream Story
Donald Broadribb (Baker's Hill, Australia). ISBN 0-919123-45-7. 256 pp. $20

45. The Rainbow Serpent: Bridge to Consciousness
Robert L. Gardner (Toronto). ISBN 0-919123-46-5. 128 pp. $16

46. Circle of Care: Clinical Issues in Jungian Therapy
Warren Steinberg (New York). ISBN 0-919123-47-3. 160 pp. $16

47. Jung Lexicon: A Primer of Terms & Concepts
Daryl Sharp (Toronto). ISBN 0-919123-48-1. 160 pp. $16

48. Body and Soul: The Other Side of Illness
Albert Kreinheder (Los Angeles). ISBN 0-919123-49-X. 112 pp. $16

49. Animus Aeternus: Exploring the Inner Masculine
Deldon Anne McNeely (Lynchburg, VA). ISBN 0-919123-50-3. 192 pp. $18

50. Castration and Male Rage: The Phallic Wound
Eugene Monick (Scranton, PA). ISBN 0-919123-51-1. 144 pp. $16

51. Saturday's Child: Encounters with the Dark Gods
Janet O. Dallett (Seal Harbor, WA). ISBN 0-919123-52-X. 128 pp. $16

52. The Secret Lore of Gardening: Patterns of Male Intimacy
Graham Jackson (Toronto). ISBN 0-919123-53-8. 160 pp. $16

53. The Refiner's Fire: Memoirs of a German Girlhood
Sigrid R. McPherson (Los Angeles). ISBN 0-919123-54-6. 208 pp. $18

54. Transformation of the God-Image: Jung's *Answer to Job*
Edward F. Edinger (Los Angeles). ISBN 0-919123-55-4. 144 pp. $16

55. Getting to Know You: The Inside Out of Relationship
Daryl Sharp (Toronto). ISBN 0-919123-56-2. 128 pp. $16

56. A Strategy for a Loss of Faith: Jung's Proposal
John P. Dourley (Ottawa). ISBN 0-919123-57-0. 144 pp. $16

57. Close Relationships: Family, Friendship, Marriage
Eleanor Bertine (New York). ISBN 0-919123-58-9. 160 pp. $16

58. Conscious Femininity: Interviews with Marion Woodman
Introduction by Marion Woodman (Toronto). ISBN 0-919123-59-7. 160 pp. $16

59. The Middle Passage: From Misery to Meaning in Midlife
James Hollis (Houston). ISBN 0-919123-60-0. 128 pp. $16

60. The Living Room Mysteries: Patterns of Male Intimacy, Book 2
Graham Jackson (Toronto). ISBN 0-919123-61-9. 144 pp. $16

61. Chicken Little: The Inside Story *(A Jungian Romance)*
Daryl Sharp (Toronto). ISBN 0-919123-62-7. 128 pp. $16

62. Coming To Age: The Croning Years and Late-Life Transformation
Jane R. Prétat (Providence, RI). ISBN 0-919123-63-5. 144 pp. $16

63. Under Saturn's Shadow: The Wounding and Healing of Men
James Hollis (Houston). ISBN 0-919123-64-3. 144 pp. $16

Discounts: any 3-5 books, 10%; 6-9 books, 20%; 10 or more, 25%

Add Postage/Handling: 1-2 books, $3; 3-4 books, $5; 5-9 books, $10; 10 or more, free

Credit cards: Contact BookWorld toll-free: 1-800-444-2524, or Fax 1-800-777-2525

Free **Catalogue** with over **100** titles, and **Jung at Heart** newsletter

INNER CITY BOOKS, Box 1271, Station Q, Toronto, ON M4T 2P4, Canada
Tel. 416-927-0355 / Fax: 416-924-1814 / E-mail: icb@inforamp.net